ON THE ALTAR

SACRIFICE

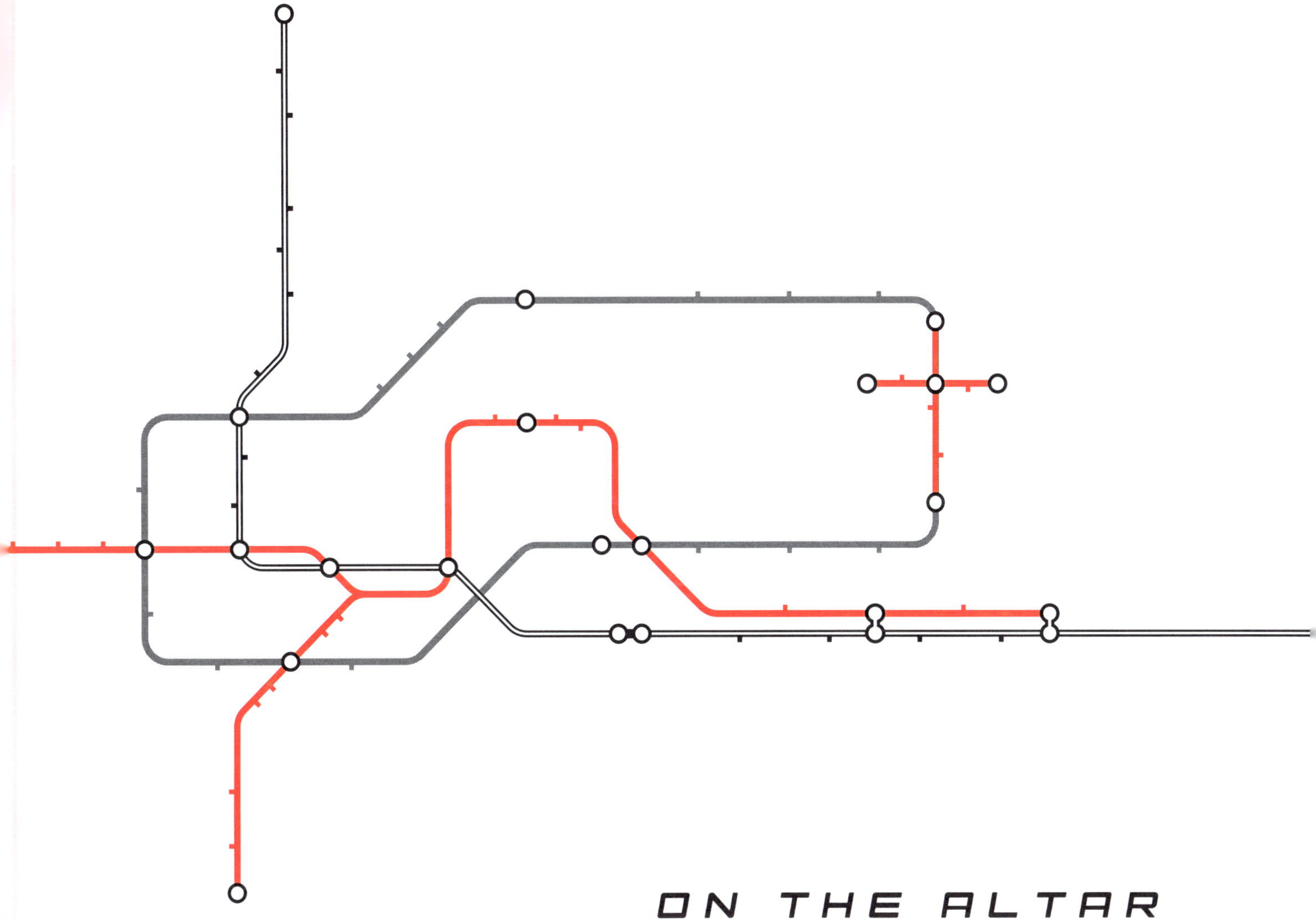

ON THE ALTAR
SACRIFICE

14 EVENT-DRIVEN STUDENT MINISTRY OUTLINES

GARTH HECKMAN
WITH JASON WETHERHOLT

Standard®
PUBLISHING
Bringing The Word to Life

Published by Standard Publishing, Cincinnati, Ohio
www.standardpub.com

Also available from the On the Altar series: *Surrender*, *Dedicate*, and *Offer*

Printed in the United States of America

Project editor: Robert Irvin
Cover and interior design: The DesignWorks Group

With contributions by Jason Wetherholt

ISBN 978-0-7847-2268-8

15 14 13 12 11 10 09   9 8 7 6 5 4 3 2 1

CONTENTS

LET'S GET IT STARTED

As a youth pastor or youth leader, how often have you had these thoughts while putting together a meeting for your group? *If I just had more time.* Or, *If I just knew how to make it stick.* You want to provide something life-changing for your students, but you also have to do it in the midst of your own crazy-busy life.

We're here to help! The On the Altar books—this book, *Sacrifice,* and the companion volumes in the series, *Surrender, Dedicate,* and *Offer*—not only give you proven outlines and relevant applications, both with a scriptural basis, they provide opportunities for memorable experiences at the beginning and end of every youth talk.

When was the last time one of your youth meetings had your students talking about and living out, and not just *hearing,* what you said? This book is about helping you get your students to the point of laying their lives at the altar.

HOW DOES IT WORK?

Each book has outlines for fourteen fantastic youth meetings. You'll have enough for a quarter's worth of meetings and an extra one to spare.

The book is broken into two halves. Both follow the *Sacrifice* theme: The first seven meetings will help your students learn the principles of sacrifice **to develop a servant's heart like Jesus;** the second seven are centered around **working through the toughest of issues and temptations** to find our ultimate identity in Jesus.

Each session starts with an icebreaker (Get It Started) that will get your students up and moving. And, in following the theme of that meeting, this activity will put them in the right frame of mind. Most of all, they're a blast! In this section, a short list (What's Needed) is provided so you can prep beforehand the things needed to make it happen. While we've given you the prep list and how-to-do-it, we encourage you to make these activities work, to make them as fun as they can be, for your group. You're a youth leader; hey, by definition you're a highly resourceful person!

After reviewing the Scripture passage that is the foundation for that meeting, we've given you a great youth talk. Again, it can't be stressed enough that, though these are outlined for you, including the text for an entire talk, you should make these *your* messages. Adjust, adapt, add, or subtract; you know what works best for your group!

We've built in For Discussion questions in different places in each unit for lots of group participation.

Another feature of these books is that we've provided places throughout these talks for you to add in your stories, style, and unique voice. We call this the Burst and Branded section.

BURST AND BRANDED

Don't worry—no one gets hurt. The idea behind this element—we've provided one Burst and Branded, on average, per every major outlined point—is simple. But it's also a key ingredient in making each talk yours, in really owning these lessons.

Burst: At this spot in the outline, add your own burst of ideas that speak directly to that part of the lesson. Maybe you have a great personal story, or a story from a friend, to bring this to life. Maybe it's a story you found online, in your local newspaper, or from one of your students' school experiences.

Branded: Here you really put some teeth into each section. How has this particular point changed you or someone you know? The key here is real, lasting change, the kind that impacts for life. These types of stories make your talks more real because your students will relate to you and see you as vulnerable.

Don't feel like you have to fill out each one of these in every section; they're there for when inspiration strikes. And though we had to put them somewhere on the page, plug in your stories wherever they work best. In other words, feel free to move your Burst and Branded stories around.

Last, in each of the outlines, certain areas have been underlined; these are particular points to pay attention to that will help you challenge your students throughout the meeting.

The Wrap It Up sections then provide a link to the closing activity, in which you'll leave your students altered . . .

WALK ON DOWN

From antiquity, altars have been sacred places of worship. In ancient times, they were used for actual sacrifices or some other means of bowing before God. More recently, they're places of worship such as the Communion table.

Maybe you have an altar area in your youth room. Maybe you just have an area near the front where you have the speaker's stand or a stage where a worship band plays. Whatever the case, the idea is to set up an area in which your students can come forward to get their hearts closer to God.

The idea behind the Altered activity is *not* to set up "altar calls" for students to come forward to give their lives to Christ—though at times that may happen. What each one *is* about is to get kids talking, remembering, and *acting on* what they've just heard. They'll leave your students with a spiritual buzz and something they'll be talking about the next day at school. And hey, these activities just might help your group grow numerically as well as spiritually.

For each Altered, we've given you a short list of things needed to make it happen. But again: These student events are yours; adapt the activities to what will work best for your group.

Along the way, we've added various ministry ideas or other options for the Get It Started or Altered activities that may work for your group.

A FINAL WORD

Take some time to go over each lesson in advance, digest them, and add your own insights. And don't worry: we've worked hard at making these as cheap as possible—we know what most youth budgets look like (pretty similar to your checkbook).

Get everything in place for the meeting, spend some time praying for the students God's going to bring out, and create an atmosphere where life-change can happen.

Most of all, have fun. And trust in the one who can leave your students permanently altered!

The activities in this book are designed for learning and having fun (a novel concept—we know), but student participation should *always* be voluntary. It is not the intention of the author or publisher that harm should come to anyone involved in these activities. (Another shocking statement . . .) Neither may be held responsible should someone become ill or injured from participating. (But hey, you're a youth leader, and despite all the crazy stereotypes, we're sure you won't let that happen!)

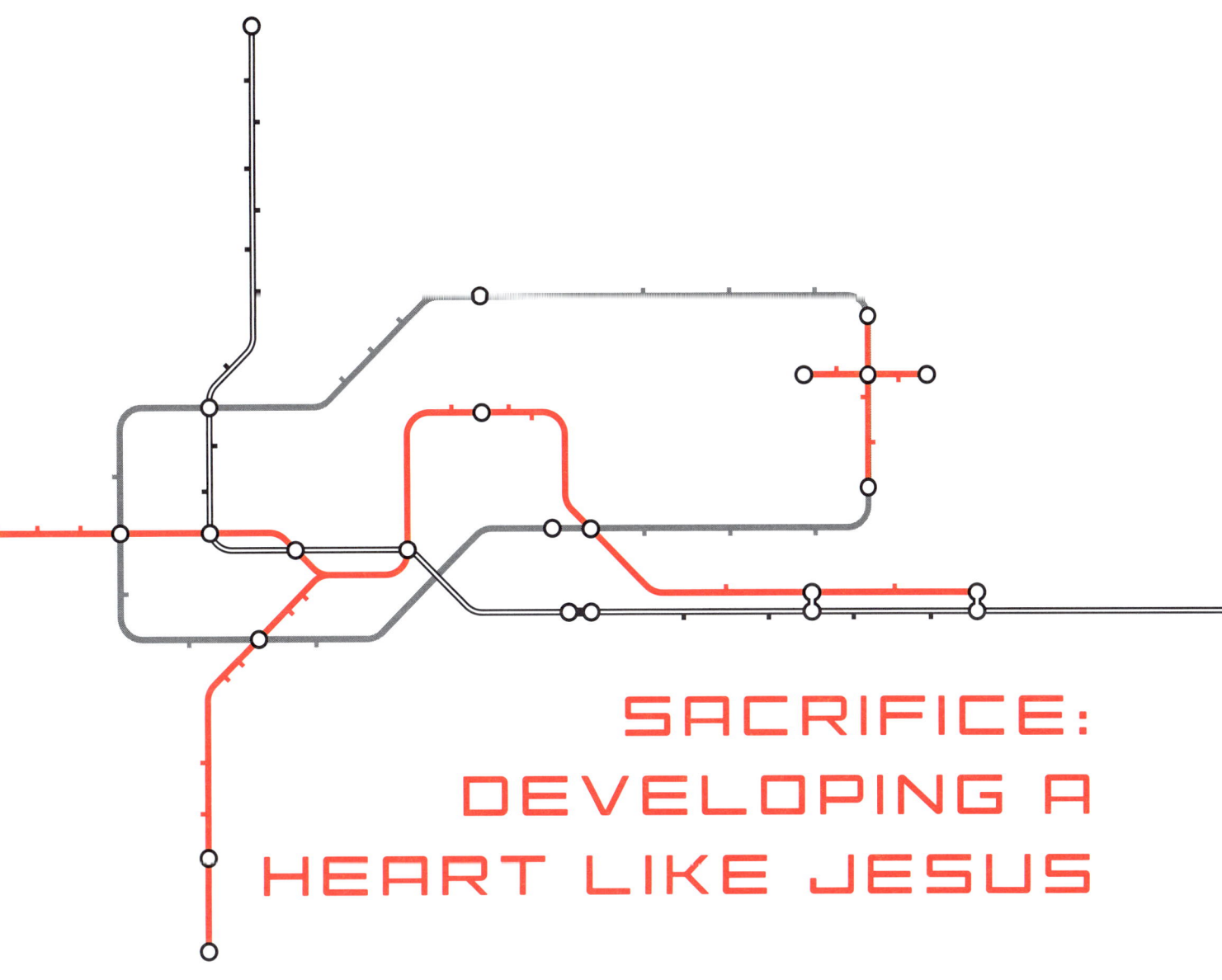

SACRIFICE: DEVELOPING A HEART LIKE JESUS

. . . YOUTH MEETINGS ON GROWING IN OUR UNDERSTANDING OF SACRIFICIAL LIVING

For to me, to live is Christ and to die is gain.

– Philippians 1:21

"The Lord does not look at the things man looks at. Man looks at the outward appearance, but the Lord looks at the heart."

– 1 Samuel 16:7

SACRIFICING YOUR FUTURE (DROPPING EVERYTHING TO FOLLOW)

WHAT IT'S ALL ABOUT

We live in an interesting time, don't we? Everything about our lives is "Go-Go-Go" and "Now-Now-Now." We expect instant success and immediate results. In fact, commenting on the ever-quickening pace of our lives, actress and theater performer Carrie Fisher has said, "Instant gratification takes too long."[1] We expect everything to come to us now, and yet . . . we always seem to push God off till later, don't we?

"I'll start reading my Bible once the semester winds down." "I'll do more with the church body once I get my license and can drive myself." "I'll go into ministry later on in life once I've made some money and established a comfortable lifestyle."

The problem is that God isn't calling us to follow when we have the time or when it's convenient; he's calling us to follow *now*. In this meeting you and your students will look at a few of the "at once" moments in the Bible.

Get It Started

What's needed: *A trough full of water and forty live goldfish* (inexpensive feeders are fine); *a bucket*; and if you're not doing this game on a surface that's OK to get wet, you'll want *a tarp* to go under everything

Students will be introduced to two important aspects of the lesson with this game: the fast pace of our lives and the fishermen who left everything to follow Jesus.

Ask for a couple of volunteers who will catch fish in the trough with their hands and put them into the bucket. Give each volunteer twenty seconds to move those fish. The winner is the one who puts the most fish into the bucket. (After each volunteer finishes, return the fish to the trough, but leave a little water in the bucket for the ones who will be thrown in next.)

Either have someone operate a stopwatch or, if you have the ability, put a twenty-second countdown clock on your screen in your meeting room. It's fun to have all students count down out loud with you when the timer hits five seconds left.

More helpful stuff: First, ask the pet store when you buy the fish about the best way to acclimate them to the trough environment. (It won't be too tough for students to catch a bunch of dead fish floating around.) Second, think through a game plan for getting rid of the fish. Does you church have a tank? Do you know someone who could use feeders? Give them to students? Then think about how they'll get them home. (Trust us who have been here before: you don't want to see the tears on the faces of the junior high girls when they find out you're just going to flush Nemo and all his buddies!)

Where It's Found in the Bible

Matthew 4:18-20

As Jesus was walking beside the Sea of Galilee, he saw two brothers, Simon called Peter and his brother Andrew. They were casting a net into the lake, for they were fishermen. "Come, follow me," Jesus said, "and I will make you fishers of men." At once they left their nets and followed him.

Acts 9:1-4, 17-20

Meanwhile, Saul was still breathing out murderous threats against the Lord's disciples. He went to the high priest and asked him for letters to the synagogues in Damascus, so that if he found any there who belonged to the Way, whether men or women, he might take them as prisoners to Jerusalem. As he neared Damascus on his journey, suddenly a light from heaven flashed around him. He fell to the ground and heard a voice say to him, "Saul, Saul, why do you persecute me?"

Then Ananias went to the house and entered it. Placing his hands on Saul, he said, "Brother Saul, the Lord—Jesus, who appeared to you on the road as you were coming here—has sent me so that you may see again and be filled with the Holy Spirit." Immediately, something like scales fell from Saul's eyes, and he could see again. He got up and was baptized, and after taking some food, he regained his strength. Saul spent several days with the disciples in Damascus. At once he began to preach in the synagogues that Jesus is the Son of God.

YOUTH TALK OUTLINE

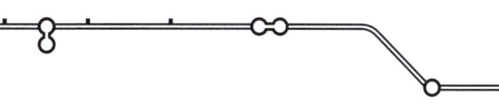

1. Slowing Down to Listen

   a. Establishing a connection

Sometimes it feels like all of our gadgets—these things in our lives that help us become "more efficient" and feel "more connected," actually create a prison for us. We're engaged in daily relationships with hundreds of people online and via text messaging, but our conversations rarely go deeper than surface level, so we end up feeling more disconnected than we did before we had all of these so-called connection tools.

      Thankfully, in the midst of all of this craziness, there is a God who wants to connect with us on far more than just a superficial level. He wants to know us. He cares about your day. He wants to speak into your future. He wants to hear and be heard. And in spite of how disconnected you might feel from others, God has never moved. He wants to establish a connection with you if you're willing to turn to him.

BURST:

BRANDED:

b. Listening up

Life is full of noise, isn't it? We wake up to a noisy alarm clock, turn on the TV while we get ready for school, listen to music in the car while talking and/or texting, and we're bombarded by "silent billboards" as we drive. Then many of us spend all day at a loud school, just to get home and turn on the TV again and spend several hours talking with others through any number of social media. Then when we finally *do* get a moment of peace and quiet, what do we do? Pop in our headphones to listen in and tune out the world.

Normally we don't think anything about this lifestyle, until someone challenges us to spend time praying and listening for God. We quickly answer that God seems distant, uninvolved, and never speaks to us!

But what if the problem isn't that God's not speaking? What if the problem is that we're not listening? What if the noise with which we've filled our lives is actually drowning out the voice of God?

FOR DISCUSSION WITH YOUR GROUP:

- Do you ever feel disconnected from the deeper, more meaningful things of life? Why do you think that is?
- Do you think your life is too busy and hurried? What can you do about that if so?
- What are the things that create the most "noise" (distraction) in your life? (For many people, these might be more than just iPods and cell phones, the first things we think of. They could be things like relationships, strained friendships, tension at home, and more.)

2. Dropping Your Nets

a. I have a dream . . .

Re-read Matthew 4:18-20. You might even want to circle the phrase "at once" in your Bible. It doesn't say "once basketball season was over" or "as soon as summer vacation gave them a little more time" or "once they had totally figured out every detail." The text says "at once." Think about that. The disciples of Jesus left *everything*.

Imagine quitting your job, leaving your livelihood, walking away from everything that formed your identity. Now, you may not be planning on bagging groceries or taking tickets at the movie theatre forever, but we all have hopes and dreams and plans for our future, don't we? The question is: are those *your* hopes and dreams and plans, or have you spent a proper amount of time asking God what *his* plan is for your life?

Our prayer lives must never be about asking God to bless our plans, but rather asking him to reveal *his*.

FOR DISCUSSION:

- Think about the phrase "What do you want to be when you grow up?" While it's cute to ask a small kid this, it's an important question that eventually needs answered by all of us. So, what is it that you want to do with your life?
- Do you sense God leading you in any certain direction? It's fine if that answer is no; absolutely fine. If it is no, be patient. God reveals things to us throughout our lives.

BURST:

BRANDED:

b. Excuses, excuses

It seems like we have an excuse for everything, don't we? If you read Acts 9:10-16, Ananias had some great excuses too. God calls him to go meet Saul, and Ananias is quick to point out why that might not be the best idea. After all, this guy is one of the biggest threats to Christianity in the first-century world. People walk on egg-shells when he's in town and pray they never have to encounter him face-to-face. It's understandable why a Christian wouldn't want to go meet with him, lay hands on him, and offer to pray for him.

But God says "Go!" and Ananias listens. What's his reward for his bravery? He gets to play a small part in perhaps the biggest conversion of all time. Saul's name gets changed to Paul, Paul goes on to write thirteen of the twenty-seven books of the New Testament, and he arguably becomes the second-most influential person in all of Christian history, next to Jesus.

What if we stopped with the excuses and simply became faithful in whatever God calls us to do?

3. Speaking Out

a. We don't need no education

Too often we buy the lie that speaking out for God is something to be left to the "professionals." The whole point of Christianity is sharing your journey with others in the hope that they might begin the journey as well. You don't have to go to Bible college to speak for God; you just have to be willing to share the story of what he's done in your life.

Paul lists his qualifications in Philippians 3:4-6. Remember, he was a Pharisee . . . the best of the best. We talk down about the Pharisees now because of their role in the death of Jesus, but in Paul's day, they were held in high regard by everyone around. The standards were rigorous, the education was exclusive, and their high-profile position was highly coveted. But listen to Paul's next statement after listing his credentials:

But whatever was to my profit I now consider loss for the sake of Christ. What is more, I consider everything a loss compared to the surpassing greatness of knowing Christ Jesus my Lord, for whose sake I have lost all things (Philippians 3:7, 8).

BURST:

BRANDED:

b. If not you . . .

If not you, then who? If not now, then when? If not here, then where?

Why would you want to wait for a youth minister to speak to your friends? After all, you're the person who feels at home in your school. When the "old people," the "professional ministers," walk down the halls of a local school, it's obvious they don't belong quite as much; they're outsiders to some extent. At the end of the day, the testimony that means something is the one that comes from a peer.

Wrap It Up

Read "Emily's Story" to your students. This is the true story of a teen named Emily Smedra, who attended Niwot High School (Niwot, Colorado), at the time.

EMILY'S STORY

It was fall during my junior of high school. I was the most nervous I'd ever been in my life, so I sent my youth minister a frantic e-mail one night.

"Please help. I don't know what to do," I began. Then I told him the following story.

I was in my philosophy class at school earlier that day. The teacher was talking about famous philosophers, like Socrates, who had been willing to die for their beliefs. We were discussing their lives and deaths and beliefs, and everything was going great until he turned the question on us.

"Would anyone here be willing to die for their beliefs?" he asked us. No one said a word, and people basically just looked around the room at each other. Without wasting any time, he took it one step further. "If you would be willing to die for your beliefs, please stand up right now in front of the class."

I slowly began to rise, and by the time I got to my feet I realized that I was the only one in the entire class standing up. Everybody was looking at me, and I was soooo nervous.

(What makes Emily's story even more impressive is that she lived two hours north of Littleton, Colorado, where just five years earlier, the Columbine shooters killed Rachel Scott for being unwilling to deny God in the school library.)

With everyone in the class looking at me—and me basically just staring at the floor trying not to shake or faint or anything—my teacher asked a question that totally shocked me.

"Well . . . what is it that you believe in so strongly that you'd be willing to die for?" he asked. "Please tell us about it."

I couldn't believe it. It's like the opportunity you always dream of getting, but when the moment actually hits, you're completely unprepared for it, and you have no clue what to do or say. I tried to answer, but my mind felt totally blank. I know I said something about being a

Christian and having a relationship with God, but I can't imagine that my thoughts were even remotely coherent.

But . . . to my total shock and amazement, my teacher said that the class would like to hear more. In fact, he said he'd give me time on Friday to explain my beliefs to the class.

So that's when I sent the frantic e-mail to my youth minister to get some ideas on how to present my beliefs in a way that would get people interested in faith and not turn them off from it completely.

I went in that Friday and told the class what I believed, and who knows what might have come from that one little class period?

All I know is this. I stood up. Over twenty people in the class, some of them Christians, and I was the only one who stood up. Now, you need to know, I'm not perfect—far from it. I messed up a bunch that year and made tons of mistakes. And I wasn't always the best leader at church or at school.

But I learned something that day. When God gives you an opportunity, you have to stand up for him. Will it require sacrifice? Yes. Is there a chance people will tune you out or think you're crazy? Sure. Did I take a risk that day? A huge one. But it wouldn't be real faith if it didn't require some sacrifice.

Maybe God is calling you to talk to someone about him or maybe God is calling you to a lifetime of service for him or maybe God is just calling you to take a stand for him in your school. Whatever the case, the sacrifice will be worth it . . . it certainly was for me!![2]

ALTERED

What's needed: Before your meeting, *print address labels with only one word on them: "open"*; have enough labels on hand for your students and adult leaders to take about *three each* so they can put them in a few different places (if possible, cut the labels apart before the meeting so students can pick them up without having to stick them to something right away)

Play some quiet music and encourage students to spend some time reflecting on the sacrifices God may be calling them to make in their lives. When they're ready, have them come to the front to pick up as many as three labels to be put in places they will definitely come across during the week. (You can suggest places like a notebook they use often, in their locker, on their Bible, on their backpack or athletic gear bag, etc.) These will serve as daily reminders to be *open* to—and look for—God's leading in their lives, regardless of the sacrifice this openness may demand.

End the night with group prayer.

A TRUE SACRIFICE (YOU WANT WHAT?)

WHAT IT'S ALL ABOUT

People are often asked whether they believe in something so strongly that they would be willing to die for it. (If you are doing this youth night back-to-back with the first unit in this book, you can read again, or reference, "Emily's story.") But as challenging as the idea of being willing to die for something is, many of us won't face that challenge, at least—thankfully—right away! What we *do* need to live up to is to begin to think about sacrifice—real sacrifice for today—as about being willing to *live* for God with the decisions we make each day.

Get It Started

What's needed: Nothing except a daring thing or two that you've done that you can briefly share with your students

It's a good old-fashioned game of Can You Top This? Start the meeting by telling your students one of the more wild things you've done. This does not include completely foolish things or things that were done in various states of sin in your life before Christ! (And you might briefly make this point with your students!)

Now ask the first volunteer from the youth group to tell their story, to see if they can "top" your little adventure. All the other students will turn thumbs up or thumbs down on the second story to see if it tops yours.

A small, final twist before the first student sits down, however: he or she must think long enough—for a few seconds or whatever is needed—to explain who or what they put their trust in in order to do that wild thing. Example: He shot one of the wildest rivers east of the Mississippi while whitewater rafting, going through a series of "five's" along the way? If he's honest, he'll admit that he put his trust in the rafting guide who took his group down the river (he would *not* have taken that river on his own).

Call more students up. The next one went bungee jumping? (Thumbs up or thumbs down from the other students?) Then she answers the second question by saying she definitely put her faith in whoever rigged the jumping system, including tying and testing the cord. Got to drive a NASCAR vehicle around an oval track at 150 mph or more? They wouldn't have hit those speeds without someone first coaching them and, likely, serving as co-driver while they took their spin.

The point: We may take risks in life, but ultimately we are putting our trust in *someone or something!* This lesson will be about the ultimate place for a person to put their trust.

Where It's Found in the Bible

Genesis 22:1-2, 6-12

Some time later God tested Abraham. He said to him, "Abraham!" "Here I am," he replied.

Then God said, "Take your son, your only son, Isaac, whom you love, and go to the region of Moriah. Sacrifice him there as a burnt offering on one of the mountains I will tell you about."

Abraham took the wood for the burnt offering and placed it on his son Isaac, and he himself carried the fire and the knife. As the two of them went on together, Isaac spoke up and said to his father Abraham, "Father?"

"Yes, my son?" Abraham replied.

"The fire and wood are here," Isaac said, "but where is the lamb for the burnt offering?"

Abraham answered, "God himself will provide the lamb for the burnt offering, my son." And the two of them went on together.

When they reached the place God had told him about, Abraham built an altar there and arranged the wood on it. He bound his son Isaac and laid him on the altar, on top of the wood. Then he reached out his hand and took the knife to slay his son. But the angel of the Lord called out to him from heaven, "Abraham! Abraham!"

"Here I am," he replied.

"Do not lay a hand on the boy," he said. "Do not do anything to him. Now I know that you fear God, because you have not withheld from me your son, your only son."

YOUTH TALK OUTLINE

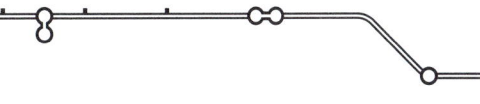

1. You Want WHAT?

a. Learning to trust

We're all control freaks, aren't we? We're taught from a very young age that we should be able to control the details in our lives. To be fair, some of those details can be good things. Parents teach us to control our bladders through potty training

. . . this, uh, as it turns out, is a good thing to control! And many of them teach us to control our tempers; that's a good thing as well. But it goes deeper than that, doesn't it?

As strange as it may sound, there was a day—and not that many years ago—in which people had no choice but to trust someone else to play the music they liked. You would turn on a radio station, hoping they would play songs you wanted to hear. But now iPods & iTunes & an *I-I-I* culture have taught us that every aspect of our lives should be customizable to our own desires at any given moment.

Cell phones and computers and other techno devices have given us a false sense of independence and control. But the irony is that what they've actually done is make us depend on and trust in them even more!

Don't misunderstand: we're not saying the gadgets themselves are evil. <u>The problem is not with our toys; the problem comes when our desire for control begins to overshadow our need for God.</u>

FOR DISCUSSION WITH YOUR GROUP:

- By a show of hands, how many of us would call ourselves admitted control freaks? Be honest—and if you feel you are *not*, don't feel compelled to raise your hand!
- What areas of your life, whether you are or aren't at that level, do you try hardest to control?
- What aspects of your relationship with God are hurt the most by your need for control?

b. Maybe Abraham's actions were only half the story

We tend to think of this story in Genesis in terms of the lesson Abraham learns when God asks him to sacrifice his son, and rightly so. After all, Abraham was a man who had many reasons not to trust God. He was asked to leave his home and his family and friends to head out and start a new nation. He was promised this nation would come through his descendants, but he wasn't even given this son until late in life. *Then* God asks him to sacrifice that very son.

But what about Isaac? It's easy to consider the boy a passive observer in this story, with no choice in the matter. But look at the details. He was able to go on a three-day trip without his mother, so he probably wasn't a toddler. He was able to be depended on to carry wood up a mountain. Many believe it's possible Isaac was in his teens—close to or at *your* age—when his father sought to sacrifice him on an altar.

Maybe this story isn't only about a dad who had to learn that his relationship with God was more important than the life of this son for whom he'd waited so long.

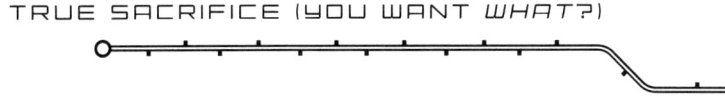

Maybe *we* can also learn a lot about trusting in our Father in heaven, even when the path before us looks nothing like we thought it would.

BURST:

BRANDED:

2. Consider the Source

a. Even when you don't understand

Have you ever flown in a plane and wondered how the huge hunk of metal that you're sitting in and that weighs several tons could actually get off the ground and then stay miles up in the air for hours at a time? It's a good thing you don't have to understand the engineering behind it in order to fly, or most of us would be traveling by bus or train (and then we'd want to understand the engineering of how those things work)! We don't have to understand every detail about something to trust it. We simply have to be willing to put our faith in the hands of the maker. Think about it: thousands of people put their lives into the hands of the makers of airplanes every day. Maybe we can put our trust into the hands of someone a lot greater than those who build planes—into the hands of the Maker of our lives.

BURST:

BRANDED:

b. Letting go

What are we waiting for? Do you have to know all "the facts" first? Have you ever known all the facts in any other relationship in your life? Do you have to have "all the answers" first? <u>Doesn't every system of belief require some form of faith on some level—even for all those people who believe in evolution?</u> Of course they've put their faith into a system of belief as well, just a different system, and one that requires faith.

Do we need proof of God? Just look around; the proof is everywhere! Now go back to Abraham and Isaac: how much "proof" did they have that God was there, listening, and still caring deeply about them? <u>They didn't have absolute proof; still, they took the ultimate steps of faith.</u>

FOR DISCUSSION:

- What do you think most people are waiting for? Why don't more people that you interact with every day trust God with their lives?
- What are some areas in which you need to let go and trust God?
- How can you do a better job of trusting him this week? What does that look like for you?

3. Trustworthiness

a. Trusting others

Trust doesn't always come easily to us, especially when we've been hurt before. Those who've been abused, mistreated, or abandoned have an especially hard time working through the issue of trust. And even if you don't have a tragic past, trust isn't always the easiest thing. Youth leaders say they care, and then other jobs carry them away to another place. Teachers say they care, and then we read stories of extreme breaches of trust. And even parents—we know deep down that they care, but sometimes their actions don't mesh with what they're saying. <u>Still, we each have to learn the truth that we were created to live in community with others, and that we will never experience the fullness and richness of Christian community if we don't learn to trust others.</u>

FOR DISCUSSION WITH YOUR GROUP:

- Why is it sometimes tough to trust other people?
- How can you become a more trustworthy person?

b. Becoming a person of trust

Unfortunately, there's no magic formula that automatically makes the people around you trust you more. In fact, the only immediate change in trust is the loss of it if someone does something that proves to be untrustworthy. Consistency is the key. We must live with integrity. Our lives must consistently bear out what we *say* we believe. That's the secret to trustworthiness.

Take a minute, close your eyes, and think back to Abraham and Isaac as they headed up that mountain. There's a thing or two we can learn about trust from them.

Ultimately, there's only been one person in human history whose words and actions were always in sync with one another. Perhaps the first step toward trust-worthiness is getting your life in line with his.

BURST:

BRANDED:

Wrap It Up

It's been said that the best proof of love is trust. If you were asked today to make a list of those you trusted most in life, it would probably reveal who you loved the most. Would God make that list?

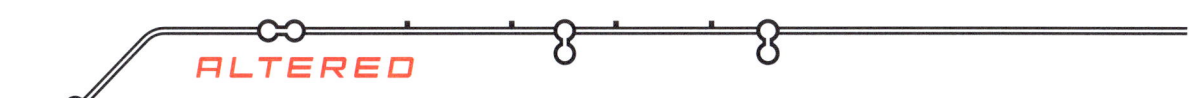

ALTERED

What's needed: *Reflective music* playing quietly; *several sets of pens or art pencils; one piece of paper for each student; one knife* (the larger the better, but care must be taken here!); *an altar* of some type (or an old table that can be carved up a bit will do)

Note: It's important you supervise the activity with the knife. Have one student at a time, with you closely watching, push their knife through their drawing into the altar or table. Another option, if you don't have that many students, is to stack the papers and you, as the leader, drive the knife through the stack.

When done, put the knife away in your backpack or some type of case. Do not leave it lying around.

Tell your students that they're going to have a chance to sacrifice on the altar whatever it is that's keeping them from trusting God. But since many of those things might cost a lot of money or may actually even be people, they're going to draw pictures and "sacrifice" only the image, the representation. It's good to be clear with your students; this isn't just arts and crafts time. If it's their cell phone that's making so much noise that they can't hear God, maybe their parents won't allow them to truly sacrifice it, but they do need to figure out how to minimize its distraction in their lives (turn the thing off, stop the texting, for periods of time). If it's a relationship that's pulling them away from God rather than pushing them toward him, you obviously aren't implying that they want to hurt the other person. The picture would not be of the other person *but of the student's unhealthy relationship that needs severed*—it might be time to cut ties or at least take a break.

Remind students that God is not looking for them to complete yet another assignment; he's expecting change in their lives. The paper is only a symbol of something larger at work. The drawing means nothing if *actions* don't change.

Give students time to draw their pictures, pray over the matter, then come to the altar to make their "sacrifice."

End the night with group prayer.

LIVING IN 3D
(SEEING CORRECTLY IN ORDER
TO MAKE REAL FRIENDS)

WHAT IT'S ALL ABOUT

Have you ever gone to a 3D movie? Pretty freaky, right? Aliens coming at you, hands reaching out, and you feel like you're right in the action. Still, as cool as that action is, most of us do the same thing at some point during the movie: we take our glasses off. It must be something instinctive inside all of us. We wonder what those images would look like without the help of our cheap, little pair of 3D glasses. And when we do, we're usually disappointed. We find out rather quickly that the images aren't nearly as cool without our glasses on.

Maybe the same is true of our lives. When we stop looking at the world around us the way we ought to, we quickly lose focus on what we've been called to do in the world.

Bill Hybels wrote a book called *Just Walk Across the Room*, in which he talked about Willow Creek Community Church's campaign to challenge people to share their faith. The idea was "living in 3D" (Develop Friendships, Discover Stories, Discern Next Steps)[3], and that's exactly what this lesson is about. But living in 3D will require certain sacrifices, as you'll help your students see!

Get It Started

What's needed: *A cell phone with a working speakerphone function; a stopwatch or something to count down* sixty seconds

Option: If you have a larger group, and you—or one of your volunteers—have a PDA phone that can be hooked into your sound system, this is even better

Also needed ahead of time: *You'll need to contact a person (or several people if you're going to allow more than one student to try this activity) whom you will call for this exercise.*

Obviously, that person needs to be alerted and ready to take this phone call during your meeting, and if you can find someone who's quick on their feet and might tease your students a little, that's even better.

Ask your students: "Who in this group thinks they can make a friend the fastest?" Bring up one student, and ask him or her if they can make a friend in one minute. Instruct the student that she will have sixty seconds to convince the person on the other end of the line to become her friend. Pull out the cell phone and call the person you've already asked to play the role on the other end. Once you have them on speakerphone (or through your room's PA system) and you've explained everything to everyone involved, let your student give it a try. This one is fun!

At the end of the minute, cut off the conversation in mid-sentence and ask the person on the other end of the phone whether or not they've been convinced to become friends.

Whatever their answer—no matter how much fun you have with this—the point of the exercise is that *real* relationships take time and effort. If the student failed to "convert" the person on the phone, the point can be made that real relationships take time. If the student succeeds, it may be a good time to remind everyone that this is just an exercise and "actual results may vary."

In truth, no one becomes a true friend in just sixty seconds; relationships take time.

Where It's Found in the Bible

Acts 17:16-23, 32-34a

While Paul was waiting for them in Athens, he was greatly distressed to see that the city was full of idols. So he reasoned in the synagogue with the Jews and the God-fearing Greeks, as well as in the marketplace day by day with those who happened to be there. A group of Epicurean and Stoic philosophers began to dispute with him. Some of them asked, "What is this babbler trying to say?" Others remarked, "He seems to be advocating foreign gods." They said this because Paul was preaching the good news about Jesus and the resurrection. Then they took him and brought him to a meeting of the Areopagus, where they said to him, "May we know what this new teaching is that you are presenting? You are bringing some strange ideas to our ears, and we want to know what they mean." (All the Athenians and the foreigners who lived there spent their time doing nothing but talking about and listening to the latest ideas.)

Paul then stood up in the meeting of the Areopagus and said: "Men of Athens! I see that in every way you are very religious. For as I walked around and looked carefully at your objects of worship, I even found an altar with this inscription: TO AN UNKNOWN GOD. Now what you worship as something unknown I am going to proclaim to you. . . . "

When they heard about the resurrection of the dead, some of them sneered, but others said, "We want to hear you again on this subject." At that, Paul left the Council. A few men became followers of Paul and believed.

YOUTH TALK OUTLINE
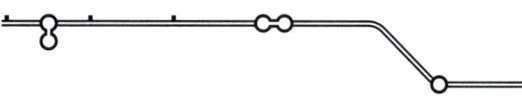

1. Develop Friendships

a. People are not a means to an end

It's important to begin any discussion about sharing your faith with a simple reminder: we don't develop friendships with people so that we can share our faith. Instead, our aim should be to honor God in all that we do. One part of that mission is being a good friend; another part is sharing our faith with the world. People are not a means to an end; people *are* the end. Paul didn't walk around Athens to make converts by force; he walked around Athens building relationships and it was then that he realized the spiritual needs along the way.

BURST:

BRANDED:

b. What about those friends?

It's long been observed that for far too many Christians, the longer they've had a relationship with Christ, the less and less friends they have who aren't Christians. And certainly, we must find a balance. If we spend all of our time with people who do not believe the same things as us, sooner or later their beliefs will begin to affect ours. But the other extreme is equally dangerous. There's an old saying: "Some Christians are so heavenly minded that they're no earthly good." Our challenge is to have enough Christian friends who can hold us accountable and challenge us to go deeper while still maintaining relationships with those who don't know Christ. Our ultimate goal with those friends is to tell them about him.

c. Just look around

We have to remember that developing friendships does not necessarily mean developing *new* friendships. God has given you the family you have, living in the house you reside in, situated in a certain neighborhood, attending your school, and you have a particular set of skills and passions and abilities which have drawn you to the friends you have for a reason. Your youth minister cannot reach them like you can, neither can other leaders, and even the rest of the students in your youth group are not the best ministers to your friends. God knew from before your birth who you would have a chance to share his message with.

Think about all the people who your life intersects with on a regular basis—cashiers, waiters, baristas, coworkers, hair stylists, teammates, those you're in band or clubs with, and on and on. You have a life full of people with whom you have enough relationship to share your faith.

The point here is being a good friend. And it's important for us to remember a few things:

• Gossip doesn't make you a good friend
• Pushing physical boundaries doesn't make you a good friend
• Criticizing Christians who are actually trying to live out their faith doesn't make you a good friend

- Walking around saying "Jesus" with every other word doesn't necessarily make you a good friend
- Refusing to talk about the most important thing in your life or refusing to talk about Jesus *definitely* doesn't make you a good friend

FOR DISCUSSION WITH YOUR GROUP:

- What do you think are the top two to three reasons teenagers don't share their faith?
- Honesty time: how many people do you think you overlook on a regular basis with whom you could be sharing your faith?
- What mistakes have you made in thinking about what makes a good friend?

2. Discover Stories

a. Life questions

Life is all about stories, isn't it? Everywhere we go, we're telling, listening to, and taking in stories. We read books because we love stories. We watch movies because we love stories. We even listen to music because we love stories, even if the stories are sometimes a little harder to find there. Stories make us laugh, make us cry, motivate us, challenge us, even inspire us.

So why, when it comes to sharing our faith, are we so quick to forget about stories? It's almost as though we think we have some sort of script to make it through, and then we can "pop the question." We're not selling used cars. Discover the stories that belong to other people. Start by noticing things around you.

Is someone reading a book you love? Do you belong to the same club? Are they using a similar cell phone? Do you go to the same school? Are you into similar fashions? Do you like the same sports? The same teams?

There's no magical seven-step process to making a good friend. We simply need to pay more attention to what's going on around us and do a better job of starting conversations that will take us inside the stories of others.

BURST:

BRANDED:

b. Faith questions

   <u>Once a conversation has begun (and probably after several conversations over time, not all in the same day), it might be natural to ask faith questions.</u> Christians are notorious for getting on the defensive rather quickly. We get peppered with questions, sometimes barraged by multiple sources, and before we know it we come to questions we cannot answer. All too often, situations like this end up making us look naive, ill-prepared, or even angry. A better strategy is asking simple questions of our own that anyone can answer without feeling threatened.

   Two of the easiest questions to ask are: "What do you believe?" and "How is that working for you?" You may find out rather quickly that a person hasn't really thought through those issues. Or maybe they've been dying to tell someone that they're wrestling with issues of faith, but they weren't sure who they could talk with.

c. Two ears, one mouth

   Once you've asked good questions, the next step is critical . . . listen, *really* listen. There's a reason God gave all of us two ears and just one mouth!

Maybe by listening you'll earn the right to be heard. It worked for Paul. He was discussing faith issues with the Jews and Greeks, and they did the nearly unthinkable . . . they asked him to address the entire council of the Areopagus, the center of where such discussions were held in his day.

By just being available, God gave Paul an incredible opportunity!

When God gives *you* the opportunity, don't back down from sharing your story and God's story. You don't have to have the Bible memorized, you just have to know how God has impacted your life.

FOR DISCUSSION:

- Here are three simple questions to think through as you think about sharing your story with others: What has God done for you? Why do you believe? What makes you go to church?

  What are some simple answers you would give to those questions?

3. Discern Next Steps

a. Opportunities . . . or boldness?

If we're honest with ourselves, we all know that small voice inside of us is often nudging us on . . . *Go talk to him about his day . . .Go sit by that girl who's alone in the lunch room . . . Don't rush off just now; just stay here and listen to him.* We just often don't want to do what that voice is saying. But that voice is very likely God's Holy Spirit prompting us to overcome our fears and reservations. We often throw up excuses like "I just don't ever have the chance to share my faith." A wise person long ago said, "Don't pray for opportunities, pray for boldness; the opportunities are all around you." Boldness is the issue for most of us. The question is not "Will they listen?" Instead, the question is "Will you be faithful to what God's called you to do?" You must be willing to give up time, open up your life and heart, and possibly even sacrifice status and popularity to be faithful to God. It won't be easy, but nothing could be as rewarding.

BURST:

BRANDED:

b. Next steps

Maybe the next step is for you to ask the person to go to church with you. Or maybe they're only ready to go to a fun event the youth group is hosting. Or maybe the next step is that they just need more time to think. Whatever it is, we need to be praying for God to make us sensitive.

Whatever you do, don't ever reject Christ on someone else's behalf. Don't decide ahead of time how they're going to respond; give them the opportunity to decide for themselves. "She would make fun of me" . . . "He'd never come to church" . . . "They'd never be open to that." Don't forget, Paul was once one of the greatest threats to Christianity; we now remember him as one of the greatest influences for Christ who ever lived.

Wrap It Up

Just remember, you are the most uniquely gifted person in the world to reach *your* friends. God has put you in that place for a reason. You're not responsible for forcing your friends to believe anything; you're only responsible for starting a conversation . . .

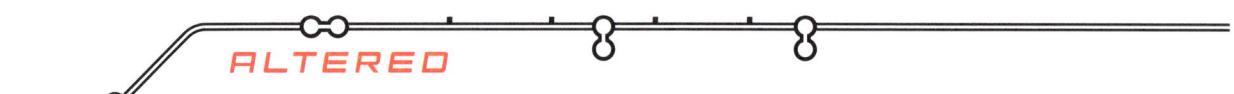

ALTERED

What's needed: Just the space to be able to break up into small groups of three or four

This lesson makes a lot of challenging and impacting points. The best closing activity you can do is simply to have your students break up into groups of three or four, share with their small group the next steps that they feel God is calling them to, and then have them each pray for the person on their right after everyone has shared.

End the night by praying for the group as a whole.

LIVING BEYOND...
(THE ART OF SACRIFICIAL LIVING)

WHAT IT'S ALL ABOUT

"For to me, to live is Christ and to die is gain." Those are pretty powerful words spoken by Paul to the Philippian church, especially considering that the guy was likely chained to a military guard when he wrote those words . . . and maybe even dictated them from his chains, because his eyesight was failing too. That's a far cry from the conditions in which twenty-first century North American Christians find themselves.

But God's expectation remains the same: sacrificial living . . . putting others before ourselves and putting God in front of it all. Let's call our students to the standard of a sacrificial lifestyle. In fact, it can be a bit of an art form—and a high calling to aspire to.

Get It Started

What's needed: You may chose to *put the following questions up on a projection screen* if you have that ability, or just read them to your group

Try an easy activity that will help your students see a bit more about what motivates them, why they do the things they do. Have everyone stand up and move to the center of the room. Then, after the leader reads (and/or projects) a question, announce which side of the room, whether left or right, you want the students to move to depending on the answer. As you and the students will quickly see, peer pressure can be a motivation in how they answer. But ask them to answer truthfully.

How many hours each week to you spend watching TV?
Less than ten
More than ten

If you just found out that work/practice got canceled, your first thought would be to hang out . . .

By yourself

With others

When you get some money, your first thought is to . . .

Save

Spend

Do you give to God 10 percent of the money you make?

Yes

No

"I have cheated on an assignment/test during this school year."

Yes

No

"I have changed my appearance or the way I dressed at some point this year based on a critical comment someone made."

Yes

No

If your mom or dad ask you to do something that's going to require a little time, you . . . (three areas of the room are needed for this one!)

Do it right away

Complain a little, then do it

Tell them to forget about it, it's not happening, then leave the room or house

When you think about your life, you would say you are:

Pretty content

Always wishing things were different than they are

Did you see peer pressure set in? You might have a laugh or two pointing out that fact, without calling out anybody in any serious way.

It's interesting sometimes how our actions really do reveal our motivations. Are we living in the moment? Are we living for ourselves? Or are we living according to a higher standard?

Where It's Found in the Bible

Philippians 1:21, 27

For to me, to live is Christ and to die is gain.

Whatever happens, conduct yourselves in a manner worthy of the gospel of Christ. Then, whether I come and see you or only hear about you in my absence, I will know that you stand firm in one spirit, contending as one man for the faith of the gospel.

YOUTH TALK OUTLINE

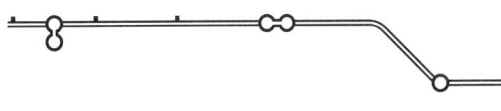

1. Living Beyond the Moment

a. Situational ethics

If you take a class in college on philosophy or ethics, you're likely going to run into this term: situational ethics. It's a phrase that's used to describe a lifestyle in which people don't think through their morals and boundaries and beliefs ahead of time. Rather, they wait until they're in the heat of the moment to make a decision, and that decision is usually made based on what their feelings or emotions tell them is best at that time.

But we shouldn't have to wait until we're in a given situation. God has given us a standard for right and wrong that transcends momentary weakness. And he's even written that standard in a book for us so that we can take it on the go. *And if we don't happen to have a Bible with us or our memory fails, then he's given us the Holy Spirit to serve as a conscience.* Our decisions shouldn't be based on momentary feelings, but rather on timeless truths.

FOR DISCUSSION WITH YOUR GROUP:

- How do you typically decide on what is right or wrong in your life?
- Are there situations in your life that are likely temptations for which you've already set a game plan?

b. A time to plan

There's a problem with situational ethics. Have you ever watched a great war movie with epic battle scenes and all kinds of fighting going on in the trenches? If you notice, there's one thing that *never* happens down in those trenches: major decision-making.

There's a reason that major battle decisions are made by generals in the relative safety of a military base or some outpost or headquarters removed from the action by a decent distance: people aren't capable of making the wisest, most well-rounded decisions in the trenches. We're simply too focused on what needs to happen next to think in terms of the big picture.

The same is true for our lives. Let's be real here: alone with your girlfriend or boyfriend with the lights off in the basement is not a time to begin forming a stance on purity. You'll find that stance pretty hard to make. Standing in a kitchen at a party you had to lie to your parents to attend is not a time to begin thinking about what your take is going to be on underage drinking. None of us do our most rational thinking in the heat of the moment. Major decisions about how we will handle certain critical moments of our lives must be made long before we encounter those temptations.

BURST:

BRANDED:

2. Living Beyond Yourself

a. What could you sacrifice?

Many—possibly most—Christians no longer practice the idea of Lent (giving up certain foods for the fifty days between Ash Wednesday and Easter). But maybe that's an ancient practice that ought to be revisited. Many Christians don't actively practice fasting; maybe we should. Giving up something in our lives allows us to pray and remember God each time we think about that thing. Maybe food isn't the struggle for you, but fasting from TV for one week would help you to see how much of a dependence you've developed on it. Or maybe, for you, it's instant messaging or your MP3 player. What if you took some time and simply stayed away from the Internet—in any form of use (doing Facebook or MySpace, IM'ing, surfing, watching YouTube, reading blogs, whatever)? Whatever the case is for you, it's clear that each of us could benefit from taking a set amount of time, dedicating that time to God, and getting rid of anything that might threaten to take our focus away from him.

BURST:

BRANDED:

b. Where could you be serving?

When we hear the term *serving*, our minds often race quickly to homeless shelters and soup kitchens. Those are great places to serve, and those ministries could not continue without the help of people volunteering their time. But at the same time, don't forget about how essential serving is in your church. What if this student ministry had a group of students who cared so much about the lost that they volunteered to come in each week before anyone else to set up chairs and get the room ready? What if there were student leaders who, rather than waiting for their youth minister to ask, were always the first to step up and willing to serve in any way they were asked?

Service shouldn't be something that requires us to schedule a time for it—service should become the Christian's lifestyle. Don't forget that when Paul wrote those words we heard earlier, he was under house arrest in Rome. And he still managed to use the words *joy* and *rejoice* fourteen times in a letter of only a few pages.

FOR DISCUSSION:

- Where are you already serving? Don't hold back on sharing ways in which you *are* pleasing God.
- What are some areas in which you're feeling called to step up and start serving more? Or to begin serving?

3. Living for the Beyond

a. Giving up

Let Paul's words sink in again: "For to me, to live is Christ and to die is gain." Paul is basically saying, "I'm with you either way, God. If you give me another day of life, I'll live it for you. And if you take me home today, I'll rejoice over getting to spend eternity with you, because that's better anyway." He's also saying, "I want to make all my decisions based on what will make me most like Christ, and most please Christ."

Could you say those things? Is your life so connected to God that every day is another chance to live for him and for his son, Jesus? Are you honestly OK with him taking you to heaven anytime, because all you want is to be able to spend more time praising him? It's a pretty high standard, isn't it? We're not used to being that committed to anything in our world, but living for God is not a part-time job. We don't get to punch a time card when we start, turning it off at the end of a work day. Living for God is an always-on, all-encompassing lifestyle.

BURST:

BRANDED:

b. Creating a battle plan

Remember the war/battle analogy from earlier? Now is the time to begin formulating your own battle plan. You have some time to think. You're removed from the heat of the battle; there's nothing else competing for your attention. Let's spend a few minutes talking about your battle plan.

FOR DISCUSSION:

- What are some of the nonnegotiables in your life? What are some of the areas in which you refuse to compromise? What standards have you already set?
- What are some areas of your life in which you're still trying to make up your mind on what you believe or how you intend to live?
- What are some of your biggest struggles in this area?
- What's your battle plan? How will you defeat Satan in the areas of your life that he threatens the most?

Wrap It Up

Making it through this life with God, and holding to faith, will only happen by establishing a clear plan, thinking that plan through, and living it out. Don't wait until you're chained to a military guard to contemplate your life—decide who you want to be today, and live like there's no tomorrow.

ALTERED

What's needed: *At least one or two links of chain for each student and adult* in attendance; *one permanent marker for every three to five people*; *set up the stations* described below in advance

Close your meeting with a time of quiet reflection. With several stations set up with links of chain and markers at them, ask students to divide up into groups of about five and go to various stations. Have them reflect on Paul's sacrifice while in chains. Ask them to write on a link or two one simple way they intend to live beyond themselves this week, to begin serving as God has called them. If you're able to get chain divided into one- or two-link sections, have the students take them home with them. If they're longer sections, keep the links and hang them in your youth room.

End the night with group prayer.

AMISH GRACE
(LOVING GRACE AND LIVING IT OUT)

WHAT IT'S ALL ABOUT

Our memory is such a powerful thing. Studying for tests, memorizing those important phone numbers, those annoying people who always seem to remember the *one time* your actions didn't mesh with what you're saying now . . . we all have truly powerful capabilities with our minds. God created us with the ability to remember an amazing amount of information, but sometimes that memory can be our own worst enemy.

Sometimes it's almost impossible to accept grace, and give it to others, because our memories seem to work too well at reminding us of the past. It's time to forget the past sins of others and our own past . . . and begin to accept the grace God is offering. We must sacrifice our memories and allow God to fill us with new ones.

Get It Started

What's needed: *Two paper bags each filled with twenty different small items that are easily recognizable by touch*—examples include things like pen, pencil, eraser, paper clip, rock, rubber band, whistle, tennis ball, watch, credit card, cell phone, iPod, piece of candy, small flashlight, puzzle piece, small cup, Scotch tape, clothes pin, ring, checkbook, sunglasses, scissors, and more; *a pen or pencil and paper* for each volunteer who serves as a scribe; *a watch with a second hand, or stopwatch*

Ask for two volunteers. One will come to the front, reach her hand into one of the bags and feel each of the items. She only gets thirty seconds to do this. (Make sure she doesn't look in the bag at any point.) Then take the bag away and see how many items she can remember. Have the other volunteer take notes and write down each item the person can remember. When the volunteer is done, take the items out of the bag to see how she did. Repeat again with a second volunteer and a second scribe. (The second set of twenty items will have to be different from the first set.)

Here's a segue opener to come out of this activity:

"Our minds are powerful things, aren't they? We remember all sorts of useful information, trivial details, and even some things we wish we could forget. Unfortunately, these powerful brains of ours sometimes get in the way when our memories do too well at reminding us of the past. Today we're going to talk about grace, and how it's the essence of the good news of Christ."

Where It's Found in the Bible

Matthew 18:21-35

Then Peter came to Jesus and asked, "Lord, how many times shall I forgive my brother when he sins against me? Up to seven times?" Jesus answered, "I tell you, not seven times, but seventy-seven times.

"Therefore, the kingdom of heaven is like a king who wanted to settle accounts with his servants. As he began the settlement, a man who owed him ten thousand talents was brought to him. Since he was not able to pay, the master ordered that he and his wife and his children and all that he had be sold to repay the debt.

"The servant fell on his knees before him. 'Be patient with me,' he begged, 'and I will pay back everything.' The servant's master took pity on him, canceled the debt and let him go.

"But when that servant went out, he found one of his fellow servants who owed him a hundred denarii. He grabbed him and began to choke him. 'Pay back what you owe me!' he demanded.

"His fellow servant fell to his knees and begged him, 'Be patient with me, and I will pay you back.'

"But he refused. Instead, he went off and had the man thrown into prison until he could pay the debt. When the other servants saw what had happened, they were greatly distressed and went and told their master everything that had happened.

"Then the master called the servant in. 'You wicked servant,' he said, 'I canceled all that debt of yours because you begged me to. Shouldn't you have had mercy on your fellow servant just as I had on you?' In anger his master turned him over to the jailers to be tortured, until he should pay back all he owed.

"This is how my heavenly Father will treat each of you unless you forgive your brother from your heart."

YOUTH TALK OUTLINE

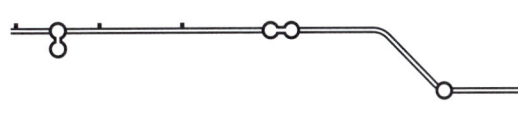

1. Asking Better Questions

a. The 'creed' of American Christianity

At the start of this story, Peter opens up the discussion with a question that we all ask in our lives on a regular basis. Sure, he camouflages his question in good, solid "church talk." But it's easy to wonder if what Peter *really* meant in his question to Jesus was "How bad can I be and still get into heaven?" In some ways, this has become the creed, the backdrop, of much of what calls itself American Christianity. It's easy to ask this question or one of its variants: "How far is too far?" "Is it really a bad thing if I . . . ?" "But what about . . . ?" "What if someone *really* deserved that thing I did to them?"

Why is it that, deep down, we want to ask God, "How far away from you can I live and still be welcomed into your family?" It's a little bit like walking out on a ledge. You creep closer and closer to the edge, but sooner or later there will come a time when you take one step too many—and find yourself in a situation you never intended to be in.

BURST:

BRANDED:

b. More like you

A better question for us to begin asking is "God, how can I be more like your Son?" "How do I get *your heart*? The heart of God, the Maker of the universe?" Not "How many times *must* I forgive?" Instead, "How can I become a more forgiving person?"

FOR DISCUSSION WITH YOUR GROUP:

- On a scale of one to ten ["1" is Adolf Hitler, "10" could represent the mercy and compassion of Mother Teresa], how much of a forgiving person are you? Why do you give yourself that number?
- When is it toughest to forgive?
- What does it usually take in your life before you're ready to forgive? Is it right that it takes that circumstance to happen first?

2. Giving Grace

a. Amish grace

Tragedy struck the Amish community of Nickel Mines, Lancaster County, Pennsylvania, on October 2, 2006. A gunman broke into an Amish school, killed five students, and injured five others before turning the gun on himself. As startling as an attack like this is anywhere—and even more so on a peace-loving group of people like the Amish—an even more unbelievable event took place six short days later. As the family of the gunman gathered in heartbroken bewilderment, they were even more surprised to see that more than half of the seventy-five mourners at the funeral were Amish.

The book *Amish Grace: How Forgiveness Transcended Tragedy* records the events surrounding the tragedy and offers some reflections:

"A friend of the killer's widow said, 'The forgiveness and generosity of the Amish had a powerful impact on Amy. She was overwhelmed and very moved by it. Many Amish neighbors came to visit her in the weeks following the shooting. They came to the burial, they brought flowers to her home, and they brought meals.'"[4]

Many who looked on from the outside wondered how the Amish could show such grace. But, in truth, the Amish couldn't imagine any other way to live.

"When forgiveness arrived at the killer's home within hours of his crime, it did not appear out of nowhere. Rather, forgiveness is woven into the very fabric of Amish life, its sturdy threads having been spun from faith in God, scriptural mandates, and a history of persecution. The grace extended by the Amish surprised the world almost as much as the killing itself."[5]

BURST:

BRANDED:

b. Lucky 7's

It may surprise us, but Peter's question was actually a bit generous. The most forgiveness that was required by the rabbinic laws of Jesus' day was actually *three* times.[6] The idea was that if someone hadn't changed their act by the third time you forgave them, then they clearly don't intend to change, and you're no longer required to offer grace. So people would have been surprised to hear Peter's generous offer of seven times of forgiveness. But then imagine their jaws dropping open and hitting the sand when Jesus replies with a standard of . . . seventy-seven times! Obviously, Jesus wasn't giving a magic number here; he was saying that we are to forgive indefinitely.

c. unChristian attitudes

- What's the first thing that comes to mind when you hear the word *Christian*?
- How about you friends at school—what do you think the word means for them?
- How do you think a typical group of non-Christians would respond if asked, "What is one word that describes present-day Christianity?"

Let's take a look at what some in society call un-Christian attitudes. Here is something that was published in the 2007 book *unChristian*. The numbers beside the terms represent the percentage of those surveyed (the audience was people between 16 and 29 who are outside the church) who said that "Christians" are represented by the following one-word or one-phrase stereotypes "a lot":

"Here are some words or phrases that people could use to describe a religious faith. Indicate if you think each of these phrases describes present-day Christianity.

66 (percent) – anti-homosexual
57 – judgmental
54 – hypocritical (saying one thing, doing another)
28 – old-fashioned
46 – too involved in politics
37 – out of touch with reality
27 – insensitive to others
27 – boring
22 – not accepting of other faiths
19 – confusing" [7]

Sentiments like this—especially if any of us have lived, or live, this way—should break our hearts. The entire good news of Jesus is based on grace. Christ gave his life so that we wouldn't have to. But somewhere along the line Christians quit living out that grace and became known for a whole bunch of other, less attractive things. Christians must turn the tide and reclaim the message of grace. We can't water down the message of what it means for someone to put their faith in Jesus, but we can begin by communicating grace and unconditional love, the same things that God once offered to us.

The unmerciful servant in Jesus' parable learned a pretty harsh lesson because of his equally harsh attitude. He forgot the grace that was offered to him—many estimates place the amount of equivalent dollars today, that he was forgiven, in the millions.

Then he turned around and refused to forgive a sum that paled in comparison.

How can we refuse to forgive a friend for some small act when the God of the univoroo oooriffood hio Con for ovory oin wc would cvcr commit?

3. Accepting Grace

a. Allowing God to heal you

Maybe you've done something really stupid or really embarrassing. Maybe you're scared to death that other people will find out. Guess what? God is a God of forgiveness. He wants to help you heal from your past hurts. In fact, he cares so much about helping you that he's put people in your lives, people who also have messed up big time and done really stupid things during the course of their lives. They may be leaders in this youth group, they may be friends, they may be family members or other people you can look up to. Whoever they are or turn out to be, God has, or will, put other people in your life to help you.

So are you ready for God to heal your past—allowing you to understand grace in the same way the Amish displayed it toward the killer's family?

b. Turning your life over

How about your future? Have you asked God to take over your life? Have you allowed him to take charge so you don't have to? You will never truly be able to be a person of grace until you've accepted it yourself.

We can stop trying to be good enough; grace is all about recognizing that God is God, and we are not. Understanding this will allow us to love grace and begin living it out.

BURST:

BRANDED:

Wrap It Up

Love grace, and live it out—that's what it's all about. But if we're focused on the wrong questions or we're not offering grace to the people in our lives or we're not accepting the grace God has given us through his Son, then we're missing out on the greatest news that's ever been given.

Love grace, and live it out.

ALTERED

What's needed: *Quiet music; volunteers waiting to meet with students* at different places around the room

This session is a heavy one, and may lead to some students in your group who just need to talk. It will be important to let your volunteers know before the session that you're going to do this closing activity, and then announce to the students that the adults in the room are there because they care about them and want to help them surrender to the grace of God, just as they have.

Whatever your students need to talk about—whether it's meeting Christ for the first time, or coming back to him, or forgiving a friend—tell them your leaders are there to help them talk things through.

Allow some time for talking and small group or one-on-one prayer.

End the night by praying with the entire group.

A MATTER OF THE HEART (RECOVERING FROM THE SUCCESS SYNDROME)

WHAT IT'S ALL ABOUT

Our lives are all about "gettin' it done." We've become a results-oriented culture. In fact, many of us will give a halfhearted effort toward sloppy results just to consider a project done and have some sort of feeling of success. It may surprise your students, but God has not actually called us to be successful; he's called us to be faithful. Achieving that may require some pretty significant sacrifices along the way.

Get It Started

What's needed: *A room with at least 25-foot ceilings* (if your youth room doesn't qualify, you'll want to find a gym or something equivalent); *one small piece of masking tape for each team* of six to eight students; *a bag of candy* for the winning team

   Important note: Be sensible and maintain control over this activity. *Have your volunteers participate so that there is someone from leadership on each team.* You leaders should use their common sense in encouraging students but also in applying oversight. This can be a great team-building exercise; it can also create an unwelcome trip to the hospital if people aren't careful. If your leadership team uses good judgment, the activity will be fine.

   This activity will double as both a team-building exercise and an introduction to today's lesson. Split your students up into teams of six to eight (even in terms of guys and girls), give one person from each team a small piece of masking tape, and instruct the teams that they will have exactly three minutes to see how high they can get their piece of tape on the wall. They are not allowed to use anything but the members of the group. They can make pyramids or stand on each other's shoulders, for instance, but they can't use chairs or tables. Be on the lookout for teams trying to find loopholes to your rules.

Turn them loose and be amazed at what you see happen.

When the activity ends, reward the winning team with the candy and encourage the other teams as well. As students return to their seats, use a segue like: "Isn't it amazing what we can accomplish as a team? I'm sure none of you thought success like that was possible when we started, but check out those pieces of tape. And now I have to figure out how I get them all down!

"That's actually how we live a lot of our lives, isn't it? We push on with all of our might toward our idea of success, and then when we get there, we're not even totally sure what it was all about in the first place."

Where It's Found in the Bible

1 Samuel 16:7

"The Lord does not look at the things man looks at. Man looks at the outward appearance, but the Lord looks at the heart."

YOUTH TALK OUTLINE

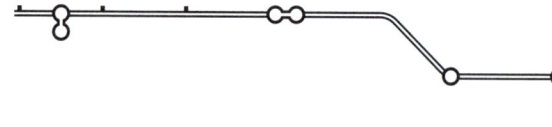

1. Feeling for a Pulse

a. Healthy heart, or heart disease?

The passage we read above contains God's words to Samuel when Samuel thought that David's older, bigger, stronger brothers should be king. God reminds Samuel that he's far more concerned about a person's interior than their exterior. The same principle is true for our churches and youth ministries. It's easy to look at a neat, polished exterior and assume that everything underneath the surface is in an equally great condition. But we all know that's not always the case.

A wise person once said, "The heart of the matter is a matter of the heart." Now, more than ever, that advice is crucial for Christians to hear. What's the condition of your heart when it comes to your definition of success? Is it time for a checkup?

BURST:

BRANDED:

b. A hole in your heart

Many of us have heavy hearts because of the past. Maybe we've been burned, or maybe we've messed up. But maybe it's not *in spite* of those things that God can use you, but precisely *because* of those things!

What was the great king David known for? He was "a man after [God's] own heart" [Acts 13:22]. But what about that whole Bathsheba thing? What about having Uriah killed? What about those whiny psalms from the caves? What about raising a son, Absalom, who tried to overthrow his father's reign? David made mistakes, but in the end his faithfulness to God is the thing he's most remembered for.

Or how about Moses? He killed a man. He tried to tell God no when God called him to lead. He took matters into his own hands in the wilderness, and God punished him by not allowing him to take the Israelites into the promised land. But what does Revelation 15:3 say about Moses as the Bible is coming to a close? "Moses the servant of God . . . "

God didn't use David and Moses to lead in spite of their past or future failures. God used them because they were able to own up to their failures and choose to live differently from that point forward.

That is a matter of the heart.

FOR DISCUSSION WITH YOUR GROUP:

- How's your heart these days? Do you have a soft heart that is open to teaching, instruction, and listening? Or is your heart headed toward hardening?
- What are the issues today that really prick your heart?

2. The Numbers Game

a. Stop playing it

How about success in how ministry is measured?

Do you think it's possible we count the wrong things? Many of us are too worried from week to week with how many people are attending the youth ministry or our church. We think our church is doing better than our friend's church down the street because we're drawing in more people.

But what if you went to heaven and found out God didn't care how many people were attending your youth ministry or church? What if you found out he only cared about the number of lives that were actually being *changed*? God's kingdom is bigger than money and membership—much, much bigger. Stop playing the numbers game; let's focus on the challenge of being faithful.

BURST:

BRANDED:

b. But realize God cares about people

For every church that struggles with caring too much about numbers, there's a church that isn't growing because they don't care enough. Numbers are only valuable when we remember that they represent people—people who need Jesus. We can't ignore that. We can't change the people outside of our church, but we can certainly work on the people who are here to create a welcoming and inviting atmosphere. We must all figure out a way to begin caring about the right things so that God can use us to be salt and light to a world in desperate need of flavor and illumination.

FOR DISCUSSION:

- Where does our youth ministry fall between these two extremes? Do we tend to care too much or too little about the numbers?
- What do you believe is a healthy balance between the two extremes?
- What do you think is the best way to judge the health of a youth ministry?

3. The Choice Is Yours

a. Checkmarks won't get you to heaven

Are you a list maker? Many of us have resorted to making "to-do" lists to keep us on track in our busy lives. That can actually be a good thing . . . right up until we turn our *lives* into "to-do" lists. Sometimes it looks like we're a culture addicted to checkmarks. *Wake up sometime before 7 a.m.*— check. *Get enough homework done to get a grade that my parents won't stress about—check. Read my Bible at some point during the day to get God off my back—check. Fill out college applications so I can go to a new place with an even bigger list of checkmarks—check.*

We move from checkmark to checkmark, barely paying attention to, let alone enjoying, the journey God's given us. Are you looking to check off a bunch of tasks or grow as a person? Your spiritual development isn't a task to be checked off; neglecting it out of busyness will affect your ability to feel successful and fulfilled in a whole bunch of other areas.

BURST:

BRANDED:

b. Choosing a career

Is your need to feel successful getting in the way of the career God's calling you to? What if God called you to do something that showed no results? How long could you stick with it? What if God's calling you to something that won't show results in the short term but will pay huge dividends in the long run?

For far too long we've pushed our driven, Type-A students toward becoming doctors or lawyers or scientists. And strong, committed Christians are desperately needed in those fields. But what if God had more ambitious, Type-A missionaries overseas? What could God do through someone who couldn't rest until an entire village in Africa came to know the love of Jesus Christ?

Wrap It Up

Success and faithfulness are not mutually exclusive. It is possible to have both, but not if success is your primary aim. With success as your goal, you are guaranteed to make concessions to your faith along the way. You'll have to if you want to stay on the success track. But if faithfulness is the mission of your life, and you continue to make that your humble aim, God will be more than happy to take your modest efforts and do more than you could ask or imagine (Ephesians 3:20).

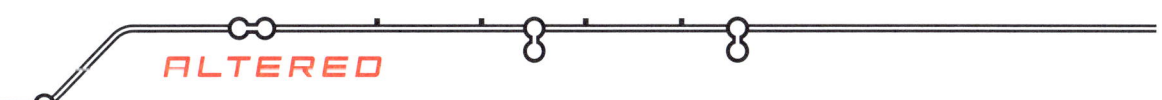

ALTERED

What's needed: *Enough pens and pieces of heart-shaped paper for each person* in attendance; *a glass bowl*

We all have faithfulness issues on our hearts today—areas in which we may be putting our dreams of success over God's plan for faithfulness in our lives.

Tell your students not to write their names on the pieces of paper. Ask them, instead, to write a short summary of one area of their life in which they're striving to be more faithful to God. Once they've written it down (again, no names!), fold the paper in half and drop it into the bowl.

Spend a few minutes in prayer with your group. Then give the following instruction to end your meeting.

On the way out of the meeting, have each student pick out one piece of paper from the bowl. In this way, they will pray for someone anonymously this week.

Together, your group can move from the success syndrome mind-set to an epidemic of spirituality and faithfulness.

TALENT CONTEST (THE SEARCH IS ON)

WHAT IT'S ALL ABOUT

We say crazy things all the time: "There's nothing I'm good at." . . . "I just don't have any talents." . . . "Well sure, I'd serve if I could be like her." . . . "Yeah, if I had his skill set." But the truth is that God has gifted all of us. And belittling those gifts or even just plain refusing to use them actually dishonors the giver. God is counting on you to take the talents he's given you to use them to change the world. That's the message you'll share with your students.

Get It Started

What's needed: *A dollar bill image, which you've enlarged and altered to look like a $1 million bill, for each person in attendance* (keep the back side of the paper blank so students can write on it); *a pen or pencil for each student*

Option: If you're graphically inclined or have a volunteer who is, you might consider working some magic in Photoshop and actually making the dollar bill look like a $1 million bill; for those of us who are graphically challenged, we'll have to resort to photocopying a ten-dollar bill, blowing it up several times, and filling in the rest of the zeros with a green marker.

Hand out a copy of the "$1 million bill" to each student. Give them a few minutes to write down the exact things they would buy or do if someone were to hand them $1 million today. Be sure to complete the exercise yourself while your students are doing so.

After you've given enough time, ask some people to share their lists. Lead an impromptu discussion as people are sharing—questions are suggested below. It's important to remember not to make fun of or belittle anyone's ideas! The whole point is to get your students to open up with this activity.

SOME DISCUSSION QUESTIONS COULD INCLUDE:

- What made you pick those things?
- Is anyone seeing any trends that were common to many of us?
- Did any of the answers surprise you?
- Did anything you wrote surprise *yourself*?
- Are there any important things that you think are missing from our lists? [Perhaps tithing, helping others, saving, other things.]
- What do you think our answers reveal?

Where It's Found in the Bible

Briefly describe Matthew 25:14-18
Matthew 25:19-30

"After a long time the master of those servants returned and settled accounts with them. The man who had received the five talents brought the other five. 'Master,' he said, 'you entrusted me with five talents. See, I have gained five more.'

"His master replied, 'Well done, good and faithful servant! You have been faithful with a few things; I will put you in charge of many things. Come and share your master's happiness!'

"The man with the two talents also came. 'Master,' he said, 'you entrusted me with two talents; see, I have gained two more.'

"His master replied, 'Well done, good and faithful servant! You have been faithful with a few things; I will put you in charge of many things. Come and share your master's happiness!'

"Then the man who had received the one talent came. 'Master,' he said, 'I knew that you are a hard man, harvesting where you have not sown and gathering where you have not scattered seed. So I was afraid and went out and hid your talent in the ground. See, here is what belongs to you.'

"His master replied, 'You wicked, lazy servant! So you knew that I harvest where I have not sown and gather where I have not scattered seed? Well then, you should have put my money on deposit with the bankers, so that when I returned I would have received it back with interest.

"'Take the talent from him and give it to the one who has the ten talents. For everyone who has will be given more, and he will have an abundance. Whoever does not have, even what he has will be taken from him. And throw that worthless servant outside, into the darkness, where there will be weeping and gnashing of teeth.'"

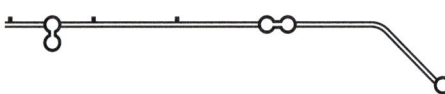

YOUTH TALK OUTLINE

1. No Equal Shares

a. The gift horse

Have you ever wondered where we get the phrase "Never look a gift horse in the mouth"? It actually comes from the days when a horse would be given by one person to another as a gift, a token of appreciation for some other action. However, sometimes it can be tough to tell the age of a horse without looking at its teeth. The idea behind the phrase, then, was that someone would look at the teeth of this "gift horse" to see how special the gift really was: did you give them a young horse or an old one you didn't care about? The point is this: either way, you should have appreciated the gesture. Never look a gift horse in the mouth.

We often do the same thing with God, don't we? He gives us all these amazing talents and blessings in life, and rather than being genuinely happy and expressing our appreciation, we immediately look at everyone around us to compare gifts. Comparisons only hurt you—never anyone else.

BURST:

BRANDED:

b. The wisdom of the giver

God doesn't mess up—ever. Maybe we need to hear that again: God has never made a mistake. He never promised to give out equal shares of talents, and he never promised to operate within the bounds of our finite, human understanding of fairness.

Is there someone who's a better singer than you? Yep. Is there someone who's better in front of people? Sure is. Are there people who are just naturally smarter? Definitely. There will always be someone better than you at everything you do. And even if you're the best in the world at something, you can still be beaten on any given day; that's why they play the games, as they say. Even when someone looks like a shoo-in, they can be beaten by someone else on the right day.

It's time to stop questioning the wisdom of the giver and begin looking for how the gifts he did give you will serve his will in this world.

FOR DISCUSSION:

- What are the gifts belonging to others that we tend to be most jealous of?
- What's the first step towards using the gifts God's given you?

2. You've Got Talent

a. How about your talents?

It's important to note that when Jesus uses the word *talent* in Matthew 25, he's talking about a sum of money that the master in the story entrusted to his servants. When we read the story, however, this key word automatically makes us think of skills and abilities. That's not necessarily what Jesus was talking about, but it is another great application in our contemporary lives. The principle certainly applies.

FOR DISCUSSION:

- What are some of your talents? And stop being modest; God has gifted everyone!
- What do people whose opinions you respect tell you you're good at?
- How are you using your gifts to serve God? How would you like to be using them?

b. How are they being used?

Think about your favorite actors, singers, musicians, athletes, and more. What would you do if you found out that tomorrow, while still in the prime of their abilities, one of your favorites announced they were giving it all up and retiring? Be honest: you'd be a little ticked, wouldn't you? You'd say: "But you have this gift; how can you neglect it? So many of us depend on you and what you create. Your gift makes us all better!"

Don't you think it's much tougher for God to watch us squander the gifts he's given us? Especially since he's the giver of those gifts? Belittling the gifts you've been given or complaining that you don't have the gifts of others or simply refusing to use the gifts you've been given dishonors the giver.

God has gifted *you* to change the world. If you aren't going for it, why are you holding back?

BURST:

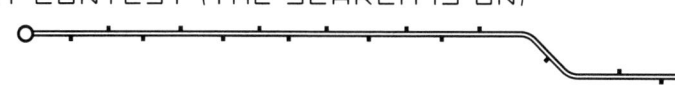

BRANDED:

3. Ready and Waiting

a. He's coming back

Have you ever wondered if the third servant in Jesus' story was actually lying? If he were truly afraid of the shrewd manager, what would he have done? He would have given the money to a moneylender to at least earn some interest. But no, he buried it in his backyard—very possibly because he didn't think the manager was coming back, and he was planning on keeping the money for himself.[8]

Ask yourself: Do I really believe Jesus is coming back? And if so, is it reflected in my life? Am I using my talents as if he is?

BURST:

BRANDED:

b. Are you ready?

How will Jesus find your life when he returns? Are you living a ten-talent life? How about a five-talent life? Have you buried your talents in the backyard, hoping never to get called into account for what you did with them? You don't get to choose how many talents God has entrusted to you; you only get to choose what you'll do with them.

Wrap It Up

One day Christ *will* return. But this won't be like a final exam where we can stay up all night and cram one last time. There are only two possible outcomes: "Well done, good and faithful servant!" or . . . well . . . how about we just focus on the "Well done!" option?

ALTERED

What's needed: *One silver dollar for each student in attendance* (or one fifty-cent piece if you have a medium- to large-sized group; if your group is bigger than your budget, you may want to go with quarters)

Hand a coin to each student in attendance. Don't have them walk up, don't let someone else pass them to the students; you hand them out. This lets them hear and feel the challenge. Their leader is passing on the expectation from *the* Leader. Reiterate for them: The call to use their talents for God are Jesus' words, not yours.

The coin is a mere representation, a reminder, for each student for the rest of the week, month, and longer.

Ask your students one final time: What are you going to do this week with your talents?

End the night with group prayer.

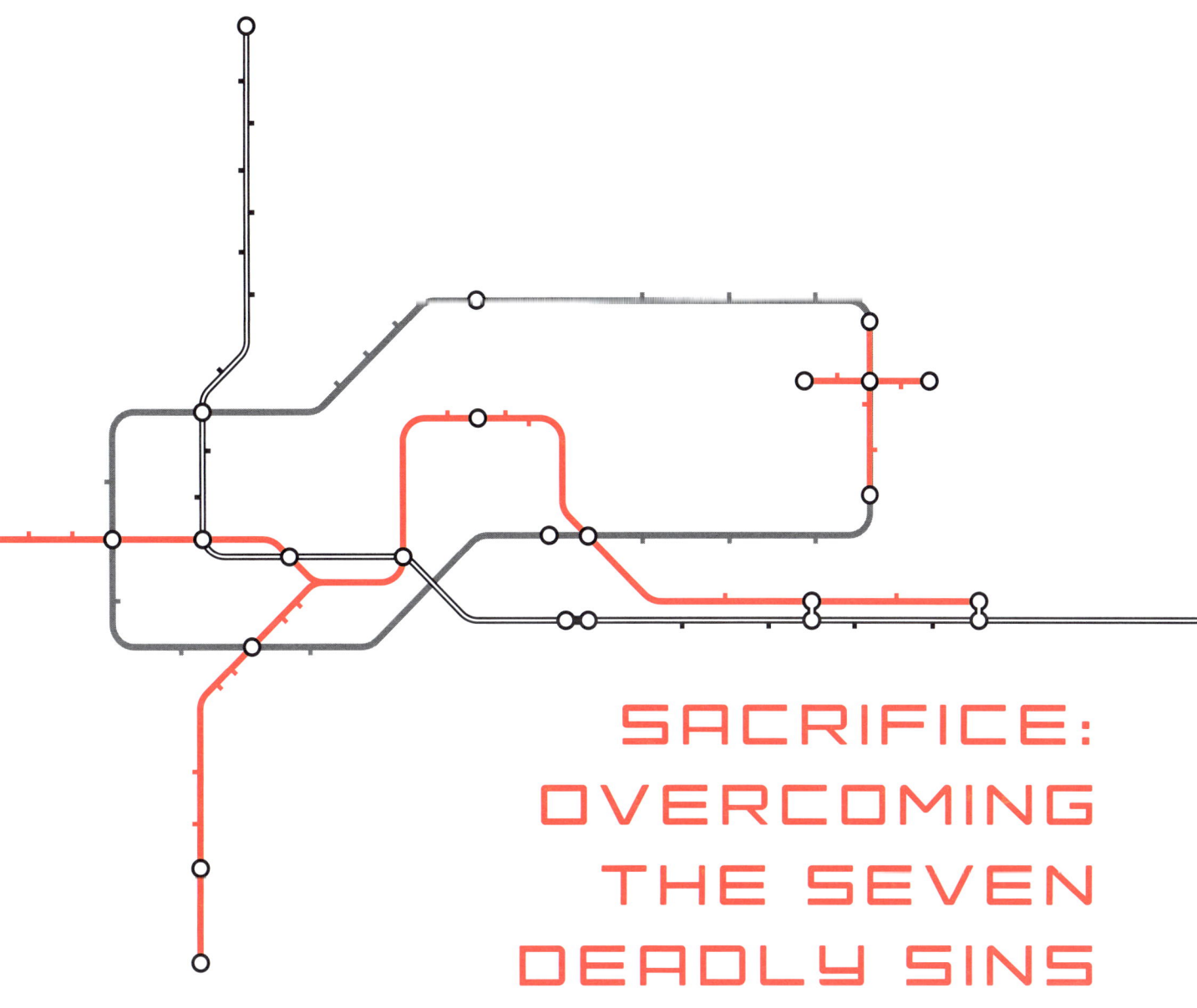

SACRIFICE: OVERCOMING THE SEVEN DEADLY SINS

. . . YOUTH MEETINGS ON OVERCOMING THE TEMPTATIONS OF THIS WORLD

So I say, live by the Spirit, and you will not gratify the desires of the sinful nature. For the sinful nature desires what is contrary to the Spirit, and the Spirit what is contrary to the sinful nature. They are in conflict with each other, so that you do not do what you want. But if you are led by the Spirit, you are not under law. The acts of the sinful nature are obvious: sexual immorality, impurity and debauchery; idolatry and witchcraft; hatred, discord, jealousy, fits of rage, selfish ambition, dissensions, factions and envy; drunkenness, orgies, and the like. I warn you, as I did before, that those who live like this will not inherit the kingdom of God. But the fruit of the Spirit is love, joy, peace, patience, kindness, goodness, faithfulness, gentleness and self-control. Against such things there is no law.

– Galatians 5:16-23

CLIMBING BRANCHLESS TREES (PRIDE MAKES US ALL FALL)

WHAT IT'S ALL ABOUT

You've certainly heard of the "Seven Deadly Sins." In the second half of this book you're going to walk your students through these spiritual land mines. (It's up to you whether you label this series as being about the Seven Deadly Sins or present these youth meetings in a different way.)

This meeting starts the list with the one from which all others flow: pride. Cockiness, arrogance, conceit, ego . . . no matter what term you use, one thing is clear: none of us is immune. This one affects us all.

Get It Started

What's needed: *Three ten-dollar gift cards* to places your students love to go (places like electronics stores, coffee shops, the local movie theatre, cool stores in the mall, etc.); *four pieces of cardstock* with numbers on one side and the name of the gift card on the other; *three useless prizes* no one would want, *each wrapped nicely in a box* (silly things like an old shoe, a ruler, a piece of paper with your autograph signed to "My #1 Fan", etc.)

Your students are probably too young even to have seen the syndicated reruns of *Let's Make a Deal*. But you aren't—so you're going to explain to them this once-popular game show and play a scaled-down version of it.

Ask for a volunteer. Allow him or her to choose any of the four cards on the table (make certain the number sides are up). Flip over their card to reveal their gift card prize and hand the gift card to the student. Then offer them the opportunity to keep their gift card or trade for one of the mystery boxes. You must play this cool, because if you nudge them toward one of the boxes, they'll be on to your game. Allow them to choose for themselves. Repeat the same process with two more volunteers.

Hopefully, one or more of your students will opt for the "bigger, better deal" and try the boxes (perhaps with the encouragement of others in the group or some of the adult leaders). If so, you have a great segue into how our pride always gets us into trouble, because we want to go our own way without being satisfied with the things we already have. If they stick with the gift cards, you have to get a little more creative. You can simply talk about how they were too smart and wise for your tricks, but if the game were played on the street (or in the real game show), people always seem to risk the good thing they already have, hoping for something better, and often ending up in disappointment.

Where It's Found in the Bible

Proverbs 16:18
Pride goes before destruction, a haughty spirit before a fall.

Philippians 2:3, 4
Do nothing out of selfish ambition or vain conceit, but in humility consider others better than yourselves. Each of you should look not only to your own interests, but also to the interests of others.

John 15:1-8
"I am the true vine, and my Father is the gardener. He cuts off every branch in me that bears no fruit, while every branch that does bear fruit he prunes so that it will be even more fruitful. You are already clean because of the word I have spoken to you. Remain in me, and I will remain in you. No branch can bear fruit by itself; it must remain in the vine. Neither can you bear fruit unless you remain in me.

"I am the vine; you are the branches. If a man remains in me and I in him, he will bear much fruit; apart from me you can do nothing. If anyone does not remain in me, he is like a branch that is thrown away and withers; such branches are picked up, thrown into the fire and burned. If you remain in me and my words remain in you, ask whatever you wish, and it will be given you. This is to my Father's glory, that you bear much fruit, showing yourselves to be my disciples."

YOUTH TALK OUTLINE

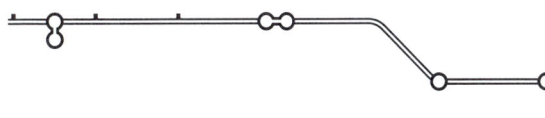

1. Pride Cuts Us Off from Reality

a. Are you in love with you?

We talk about love all the time. "I'm *sooo* in love with him." "She's the love of my life." "They're in love." But we don't really mean *love*, do we? What we usually mean is infatuation. We're infatuated with so many things in life—that is, in love with them for a short period of time, and then we move on to something else. Sometimes it seems like the only long-lasting love relationship in our lives is with . . . ourselves.

It can show up in our actions, our thoughts, our speech. We find out someone on the team got hurt, and our first thought is how much more playing time we might get. Someone talks badly about one of our friends and rather than stick up for that person, we join in because we're just glad it's finally not us they're talking about. And even when we're talking nicely about others and sounding like the most kind-hearted person around, we can't help but use words like *I*, *me*, and *my* all the time. Let's be extremely honest: It's too easy to be in love with ourselves.

FOR DISCUSSION WITH YOUR GROUP:

- What are some areas of your life in which this is true for you? Where do you tend to look out for yourself rather than for others? (**Note:** Draw out answers, but help the overall tone remain positive. Keep the discussion moving fairly quickly and don't allow it to become focused on one person belching out a great deal of sin.)
- Name one or two great examples of people you know who are often truly self-less. Tell us why you named those people.

b. Roll out the red carpet

Here's the big problem with being in love with ourselves: when we're consumed with self, we might as well roll out the red carpet—like they do before awards shows or movie premieres—and invite Satan into our hearts. Medieval theologian Thomas Aquinas once said of our pride that, "inordinate love of self is the cause of every sin."[9]

Your own ego is the only foothold Satan needs to climb into your heart. Once we fall in love with ourselves, we open our lives up to every other sin available. The reason: whether consciously or subconsciously, we begin making our very self our own god. We must build up walls to protect our heart and keep Satan out; otherwise, we begin to lose touch with reality and create our own. That's the lie that pride sells to us all.

BURST:

BRANDED:

2. Pride Cuts Us Off from Relationships

a. Destined for failure

Picture being married someday. You're madly in love with this person, who is also your best friend. You've chosen to spend your life with him or her. Things are going so well that you come home one day and announce that from this day forward no further communication will be necessary. You're already in love; you both know that. So why continue needlessly talking about it?

I'm guessing that, even in your daydream, your spouse is not responding very kindly to this information. Why? Because if you're in a relationship with someone, you want to spend more time with that person and communicate more, not less.

But unfortunately, that's exactly what pride does: it cuts us off from some of the people we care about the most. Sometimes that's because *I'm* focusing too much on *me* to care about *you*, and sometimes it's because a prideful attitude can be so offensive that people don't actually want to be around us all that much!

BURST:

BRANDED:

b. Growth doesn't have to take a miracle

If you want your relationships to be the best they can be, it begins with sacrificing your pride on the altar of humility. You were created for community. You were made for relationships. You've been wired in such a way that your heart longs to connect with the hearts of others, and if pride is all that stands in the way, then it's time to get moving.

All of us are either growing closer to others or withering away. Nothing living on this planet is able to stay stagnant. God calls us to lay down our pride and pick back up our relationships. This decision will affect everything else in our lives—especially our relationship with God.

3. Pride Cuts Us Off from God

a. Climbing branchless trees

Imagine trying to climb a tree in your backyard without any branches. Pretty tough, huh? What if you were thirty feet up in a tree and someone began cutting off branches from the ground up? It's not going to take too long before you'll come crashing down, huh? That's a great metaphor for pride in our relationship with God.

It starts with us thinking of ourselves more highly than we ought to—Romans 12:3 is a great reference for this—and then, before we know it, we're like the vine Jesus was talking about in the verses we read earlier: "No branch can bear fruit by itself; it must remain in the vine." When we tell God we no longer need him, we begin cutting off the branch we're standing on. The only way we can bear fruit, the only way we can become all that God has called us to be, is if we commit ourselves to sacrifice our pride on the altar of humility.

FOR DISCUSSION:

- What is your biggest struggle with pride?
- What would it look like for you to give it up to God and live a more humble life?

b. Who are you sold out to?

"No one can serve two masters. Either he will hate the one and love the other, or he will be devoted to the one and despise the other."

These are the words Jesus used in Matthew 6:24. To whom are you sold out? Yourself or God? When push comes to shove, we all have to choose one over the other. That's how life works. When we're "all about" two very different things, sooner or later those two things will come into conflict with one another.

It's our choice. Who will we serve?

BURST:

BRANDED:

Wrap It Up

What is your pride cutting you off from? Reality? Are you seeing correctly? Relationships? Do you need to go back and make amends with some friends or family members? God? He's ready and waiting. Don't let your pride cloud your judgment any longer; do whatever it takes to lay it down.

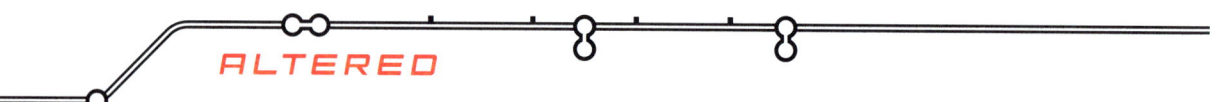

ALTERED

What's needed: *A six-to-eight-inch piece of branch for each person in attendance*

Tell your students that it's time to stop climbing branchless trees; it's time to connect with the vine, the source of every good and pleasing gift in our lives.

Invite those who want to respond to come to the front of the room and spend a few moments of quiet reflection before God. (Gently remind your students that every person has pride in different ways and nearly everyone will end up coming forward.)

Tell your students to ask God to help them cut the pride from their lives. Then have them take a branch as a reminder that we must stay connected to the vine or we'll eventually give in to pride and wither away from the faith.

End the night with group prayer.

BUFFET-STYLE LIVING (OVERCOMING A CULTURE OF CONSUMPTION)

WHAT IT'S ALL ABOUT

We've become a culture of consumers. We eat too much, we indulge too much, and on the rare occasion that we are told no, we instinctively react because we don't think we got something that we truly deserved. Unfortunately, our consumption has made us fat . . . and our waistlines are only just one part of the problem. Overcoming the gluttony that pervades our lives will require sacrifices that, for many, may be new ones.

Get It Started

What's needed: *The following food items:* one jar of creamy peanut butter, one jar of cherry jam, one can of cashews, one small bag of pistachios, one jar of peanuts, two cans of pineapple, two jars of maraschino cherries, four bags of microwave popcorn; *cups or plastic bowls* to hold each of the items; *plastic spoons and forks* for serving

A little more prep: Set up this activity ahead of time on a table in the front of the room. It's wise to cover the table with a sheet so your students don't see the food items. Oh, and don't forget to pop the popcorn ahead of time or you'll have a very difficult popcorn-eating contest!

Important: These are *not* blind food-eating contests. Due to the prevalence of food allergies today, it's important that you only get volunteers, students who say they love these foods. And that's part of the allure and fun to this game; your teens who come up must have the attitude that they can't wait to chow down on this food.

Still one more note about prep: Be sure not to talk about the gross stuff until *all* the eating battles are done. If you spill the beans on the first contest, you won't get any more volunteers. (Follow all the rules for this one and you'll find out this game is a blast!)

The activity: in two words, we're talking eating contests! Tell your students they're going to find out who can eat various foods the fastest. OK, here are the battles:

Peanut butter vs. jelly!—"We need two contestants who each love PBJs. One will get a cup of peanut butter, the other will get a cup of cherry jam." (Tip: give a little more to the jam eater, since peanut butter is quite a bit tougher to eat fast!) Put the food in front of your students and then . . . "Ready, set, chow down!"

Nutty contest!—"We need three volunteers: one who loves cashews, one who loves pistachios, and one who loves roasted peanuts." Bring them to the front, and see who can eat the contents of their cup of nutty food first.

Canned fruit—"We need two volunteers: one who loves pineapple and one who loves maraschino cherries." Bring them up and have 'em face off!

Popcorn battle—"Everybody loves popcorn, right? We need four volunteers. Each gets a bag of popped microwave popcorn. We'll see who has the least left after 45 seconds."

The real twist still lies ahead in this game. Segue with some chatter like:

"It's amazing how much we can eat, isn't it? You've probably never sat down to see if you could eat a whole cup of peanut butter or pistachios, but we consume quite a bit every day, don't we? The only problem is that we're not always the most critical consumers of the stuff we're taking in. Movies, music, food—we just don't always pay attention to the hidden stuff we take in along with the good stuff.

"So how about food? We've got some statistics for you. You go to the grocery store, you expect that someone is looking out for you, making sure to uphold strict standards for the food you buy. Did you know that the government indeed *does* have some standards? No doubt, you'll be relieved to hear that the government closely monitors how much . . . insect filth, rancid nuts, and mold is sold to you in your food.

"We are not kidding. Here are some quick facts on how many 'defects' the government allows in the foods you eat. It allows *no more than*:[10]

Peanut butter
Insect filth: an average of 30 or more insect fragments per 100 grams
Rodent filth: an average of one or more rodent hairs per 100 grams
Grit: gritty taste and water insoluble inorganic residue is no more than 25 milligrams per 100 grams

Cherry jam
Mold: the average mold count is no more than 30 percent

Nuts from trees
Multiple defects: reject nuts (insect-infested, rancid, moldy, gummy, and shriveled or empty shells) as determined by macroscopic examination at or in excess of the following levels:
Cashews: no more than 5 percent
Pistachios, unshelled: 10 percent
Pistachios, shelled: 5 percent

Roasted peanuts
Multiple defects: an average of 5 percent or more kernels by count are rejects (insect-infested, moldy, rancid, otherwise decomposed, and dirty)
Insects: an average of no more than 20 whole insects or the equivalent in 100-pound bag siftings

Canned pineapple
Mold: average mold count is no more than 20 percent
or: the mold count of any one subsample is no more than 60 percent

Maraschino cherries
Insect filth: an average of no more than 5 percent of pieces are rejects due to . . . maggots (yes, maggots!)

Popcorn: no more than . . .
Rodent filth: one or more rodent excreta pellets are found in one or more subsamples, and one or more rodent hairs are found in two more other subsamples
or: two or more rodent hairs per pound and rodent hair is found in 50 percent or more of the subsamples
or: 20 or more gnawed grains per pound and rodent hair is found in 50 percent or more of the subsamples

So, maybe we need to pay closer attention to the things we're taking in every day, huh?!
Let the groans die out and then move into your lesson.

Where It's Found in the Bible

Proverbs 23:20, 21
Do not join those who drink too much wine
*   or gorge themselves on meat,*

for drunkards and gluttons become poor,
and drowsiness clothes them in rags.

YOUTH TALK OUTLINE

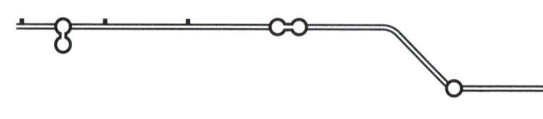

1. Control Freaks

a. Never in control . . . in the first place

Would it surprise you to hear that a large part of the consumption epidemic present in our society today is due to our control freak nature? We get hurt by the actions of others, and when we realize we can't control them, something interesting happens in the deep recesses of our minds—we go into a sort of hyper-control mode over our lives. Some of us belittle ourselves, some of us go on the attack against those closest to us, and some of us eat. Whether or not we're even conscious of it, something deep inside is crying out, reacting to the fact that we just realized we don't get to be in control of everything. The trick is learning ahead of time that we never were in control in the first place.

FOR DISCUSSION WITH YOUR GROUP:

- What are some of the biggest "control freak" areas of your life?
- How do you respond when it feels like the world around you is out of control? What is your coping mechanism?
- How does that work out for you?

b. The only proven winning strategy: giving up

The reality that the Bible teaches us is that . . . *we are not in control.* But there's plenty of good news in that little fact. And that's that we don't *have* to be in control. That should be one of the most freeing statements we could ever hear.

There is a God who is all-knowing and all-powerful, and he can be trusted to be in control of the world so that we don't have to be. Jesus said (Matthew 16:24, 25):

"If anyone would come after me, he must deny himself and take up his cross and follow me. For whoever wants to save his life will lose it, but whoever loses his life for me will find it."

We must relinquish control if we want to be followers of Christ. This is the world Jesus walked in: one of sacrifice for the good of others. One of giving up all control to come to earth to die for us. This is the heart God wants us to begin to imitate.

BURST:

BRANDED:

2. Watching What We Eat

a. How are you eating?

Over-consumption is a problem in lots of ways in our society. But let's face it: food really *is* an issue for many people. One study, titled "Fat Is the New Normal," offers the "social multiplier theory." The basic idea is that fifteen years ago people weighed less and their ideal weight also was a lower figure. But now that we look around and see heavier people all around us, we assume it's OK to gain a few more pounds, or at least we're comfortable with them once we gain them. Too many see this as the new normal[11].

First Corinthians chapter 6 reminds us to honor God with our bodies because our bodies are actually temples of God's Holy Spirit. Obviously, that doesn't mean that we have to look like supermodels. It also doesn't mean that allowing your weight to become an obsession is healthy. What it all comes down to is we have to realize that we are not the ones in charge. God was gracious enough to give us our bodies; it's our responsibility to honor him with that gift.

FOR DISCUSSION:

- What do your actions with food communicate to God? Care or selfishness? (**Note to leader:** It's an important topic and one not to shy away from. However, you want to keep these responses general. Heavier students should not be made to feel belittled in any way. Keep the discussion positive. Leave the deeper discussion on this for one-on-one counseling and discipleship times.)
- How could you be eating healthier?

b. Consuming good things

Back to the bigger issue of the all-pervasive consumption happening in our society. We all need some things, right? For example, we need clothes, don't we, or they'll lock us up. There is nothing wrong with having clothes and even some nice clothes!

But think about all the money we spend selfishly each week or each month—iTunes, DVDs, fast food restaurants, coffee shops . . . we spend a *lot*, don't we? To be fair, there's nothing wrong with enjoying a few chicken nuggets or a Caramel Macchiato. What *is* sinful is thinking only about our needs when there's a hurting world out there, desperately crying out with needs we could easily meet if we just spent less on us.

What if you cut just ten dollars each month out of your consumption? What else could you do with that money? Spending one dollar less each day would allow you to sponsor a child somewhere else in the world. Saving just five dollars each week would give you more than $250 extra this year that could be used to make a difference. Small sacrifices by us could make a world of difference for someone else. Isn't this the heart Jesus displayed?

BURST:

BRANDED:

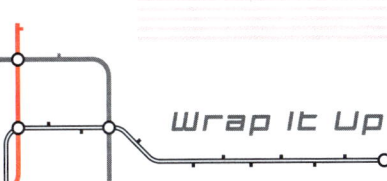

Wrap It Up

None of us is immune from the battle with gluttony. Even if food isn't our issue, we all struggle with the desire to consume. The challenge of this meeting is to let go. It's time to focus on how we can meet the needs of a starving world.

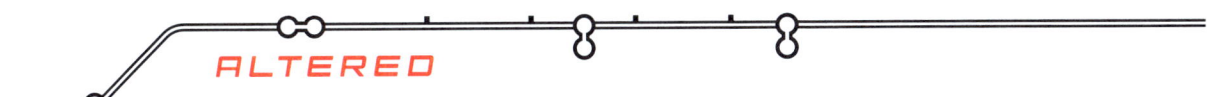

ALTERED

What's needed: *A wooden cross* that can be stood in the middle of your meeting room

The best ending for today's meeting is to discuss, as a group, the good we can be doing in this world. Turn from the points about consumption to a closing focus on how you can help change lives for the better.

Have all your students sit in a circle around the cross. Begin a discussion on this topic; following are some questions that may help get you started.

Be sensitive to God's leading during this time.

FOR DISCUSSION:

- What are some ways we could lower our consumption and raise our generosity?
- How could our group do a better job of meeting needs both in our community and around the world?
- Discuss specific strategies.

End the night with group prayer.

CLEANING THE LENS (DEFEATING THE DISTORTION OF ENVY)

WHAT IT'S ALL ABOUT

We've all seen those classic movies in which a sophisticated couple is sitting in a nice restaurant deciding what to order. Suddenly one of them looks up to see what a waiter is bringing to the next table and then utters those famous words: "I'll have what she's having."

While there's nothing wrong with being indecisive over lunch, there is a problem when that becomes a lifestyle. Envy has become such a part of our lives that we barely even notice it anymore; we just know that we're not happy. Marketers no longer tell us *why* we need something; they simply show us how happy other people seemingly are just by having their product.

When the sin of envy is allowed to creep into our lives, it begins to distort our ability to enjoy the blessings God has given us.

Get It Started

What's needed: *Enough gifts for each of your students who volunteer* for this game to have one—the illustration will be even more effective if a few of the gifts are cool things while most are useless junk (ideas: a couple of gift cards vs. an old sock, ratty old stuffed animal, rusty tools, roll of toilet paper, souvenir cup from your kitchen cabinet, etc.)

More: Be sure either to wrap the gifts or put them into gift bags. If you have a smaller group, allow everyone to play. If you have a larger group, ask for eight to twelve volunteers who will come up front to play in front of everyone.

Option: Another way to handle this is to announce a week ahead of time that you're having a White Elephant Gift Exchange; have each student bring a gift.

The activity: have your volunteers form a circle with their chairs, placing the gifts in the center of the circle. (Be sure there is an equal number of gifts and contestants.) If you're not aware of how White Elephants work, here is one variation: have one student pick out a gift and unwrap it. Then begin to move around the circle clockwise. Each student has the option of picking up a new gift from the center or "stealing" a gift from someone who's already taken their turn. If your gift is stolen, you then have the option of stealing someone else's gift or picking up a new one from the center. The catch is that each gift may only be stolen three times. (After the third time a gift has been taken, it's out of play and remains with the last person who took it.) Go around the circle and then allow the person who went first to go one last time since they weren't given the option of stealing on their first turn. The game is ended and people are stuck with whatever gift they have. (Again, this is an even more effective illustration if there are a few nice gifts that everyone wants to steal.)

Here's a possible segue into the Scriptures and the lesson:

"Isn't this a great illustration of our lives? It doesn't really matter how good the gift in our hands is, we're always looking around at what everyone else has. Even the people who drew something really nice from the unopened gifts were quick to compare their gift to everyone else's. That's our envy taking over, and it's exactly what we're going to be talking about today."

Where It's Found in the Bible

Proverbs 14:30

A heart at peace gives life to the body,
but envy rots the bones.

Genesis 4:1-12

Adam lay with his wife Eve, and she became pregnant and gave birth to Cain. She said, "With the help of the Lord I have brought forth a man." Later she gave birth to his brother Abel.

Now Abel kept flocks, and Cain worked the soil. In the course of time Cain brought some of the fruits of the soil as an offering to the Lord. But Abel brought fat portions from some of the firstborn of his flock. The Lord looked with favor on Abel and his offering, but on Cain and his offering he did not look with favor. So Cain was very angry, and his face was downcast.

Then the Lord said to Cain, "Why are you angry? Why is your face downcast? If you do what is right, will you not be accepted? But if you do not do what is right, sin is crouching at your door; it desires to have you, but you must master it."

Now Cain said to his brother Abel, "Let's go out to the field." And while they were in the field, Cain attacked his brother Abel and killed him.

Then the Lord said to Cain, "Where is your brother Abel?"

"I don't know," he replied. "Am I my brother's keeper?"

The Lord said, "What have you done? Listen! Your brother's blood cries out to me from the ground. Now you are under a curse and driven from the ground, which opened its mouth to receive your brother's blood from your hand. When you work the ground, it will no longer yield its crops for you. You will be a restless wanderer on the earth."

YOUTH TALK OUTLINE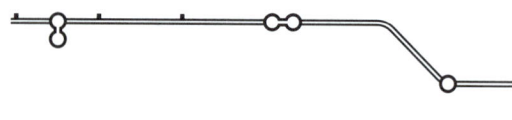

1. Envy Distorts Our Vision

a. Where's the love?

Older siblings can probably relate to this story better than anyone else. Adam and Eve had one kid, life was good, why mess it up by having others, right? With the birth of Abel jealousy, family fights, and sibling rivalry entered the picture. We've all been angry at a brother or sister, right? "Mom gave them something I wanted." "Dad let them go with him on a trip." "She ate my candy bar." "He looked at me wrong." But did we hear the words of this story?

Cain became so filled with envy that he killed his brother. That's a significant jump from two kids who push each other around in the playroom over a toy they both want. But that's what envy does. It drives a strong wedge between you and those closest to you in life. Envy blurs the vision to the point that we stop thinking, seeing, and acting clearly.

FOR DISCUSSION WITH YOUR GROUP:

- What are some of the things you have envied?
- Has envy ever distorted your vision? Share what happened.
- How can a Christian teen prevent envy from taking over his or her heart and mind?

b. Cleaning the lens

Have you ever watched a sporting event (or any kind of live event) on TV where the lens of the camera has a few drops of rain on it, and no one seems to care enough to clean it off? It starts as a bit of a nuisance, and we think, *Hey, somebody ought to clean that lens off.* And then, sooner or later, it's as though you can see nothing else other than the raindrops no one is dealing with! Here is this great sporting event or news report that you chose to watch (rather than a thousand other things you could be doing with your time), and yet you see nothing other than the few raindrops on the screen.

Envy blinds in just about the same way. No one sets out to kill a brother or sister—guarantee it. No one plans to sell out a best friend. No one intends to wish

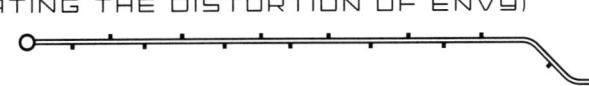

bad luck on those around them. We simply start by noticing what others have. Then we forget all the great things we've already been given. Jealousy turns to envy, and envy becomes bitterness. It's time to clean the lens and begin seeing clearly

BURST:

BRANDED:

2. Envy Distorts Our Joy

a. What's it take to be content?

Here's a good question for reflection: how much money would it take for you to be content? Now what if you got that amount of money, the figure that just popped into your head? Would you really be content? The answer, for many—if they were honest—would be "with just one more dollar."

We're unhappy with what we already have, so we assume that "just one more" *will* make us happy. Then we get to that "one more" level, and we see that still more is possible. So we set our sights on those things.

There's a portion of such drive that is healthy in life. But that portion has to do with the drive to help or inspire others. We have light bulbs and medical advances and world record sports achievements because of extraordinary people who refused to settle. <u>Drive and determination are not the problems. Our lack of contentment with what God's given us is the problem.</u>

BURST:

BRANDED:

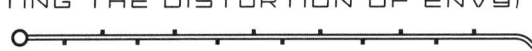

b. It's not the type of offering

It's amazing how Cain completely misses the point in the story. His envy over how God looks at both offerings prevents him from seeing why Abel's was good; he can only focus on the fact that his wasn't. God wasn't playing favorites. If anything, firstborns in the Old Testament tend to be favored. God didn't reject Cain's offering because it wasn't a blood offering; plenty of other types of offerings were accepted in the Old Testament. After all, God's probably the one who gave the work orders. He was glad to have one person in charge of the crops and another in charge of the livestock; both were needed.

No, Genesis tells us that Abel brought his best (from the firstborn of his flock), and we have no such record of Cain's offering. Abel gave his best, <u>Cain held back.</u> <u>A rational reaction would have been to take this as a learning experience and work</u> <u>harder the next time.</u> Instead, Cain allowed jealousy to take over his heart and mind. The envy that welled up in him distorted his vision, and he ended up taking out his rage on his only brother, a result that sent Abel to a very early grave.

FOR DISCUSSION:

- What are some current events in our world today that were caused by, or are being caused by, envy?
- Are there areas of your life in which you're not giving God your best because you're jealous of others? What are they? Why?

3. Envy Distorts Our Worship

a. Even in church?

Sadly, our jealousy isn't limited to the material possessions of friends, is it? At times we even allow envy to threaten our worship. Imagine this scenario: you discover that a friend of yours has a much better devotional life than you. He reads his Bible every day, his prayer life is solid, and it's obvious when he speaks his words come from a place of spiritual maturity. So you do the only rational thing you can think of—you steal his Bible and hide it. Then you find out when he typically prays each day, and you bombard him with text messages during that time. Sounds pretty stupid, right?

But isn't it easy to do things in the same vein? We see people with their hands raised in worship, and we make fun of them, because our hearts aren't connecting with God in the same way. Someone bows their head in the lunchroom to pray, and we roll our eyes when all we really want is to have the same boldness. Or someone is answering all the questions during youth group and asking really good ones too, so later we make fun of them for trying to be a "super Christian."

The truth is that we're jealous. It's the wrong spirit, a spirit entirely unlike that which Jesus came to give us.

Envy can quite easily distort our worship.

FOR DISCUSSION:

- How can Christian teens do a better job of encouraging one another's faith rather than tearing down?

  . . . Spend a few minutes on this one. Let students think, talk, and react in a positive way to this challenge.

b. An audience of One

When your life is over and you stand in judgment, you won't have an audience of five hundred (maybe the number in your high school or church) or fifty (perhaps the number in your youth group) or even five (maybe the number in your family). You'll stand alone before an audience of One. Each of us will be accountable for how we lived our lives.

So why shouldn't we start living like that now? Why not ignore the audiences of five hundred or fifty or five and begin living for the audience of One?

BURST:

BRANDED:

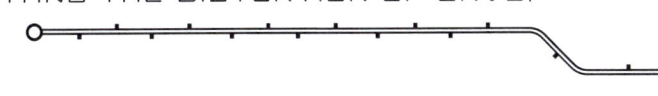

Wrap It Up

Did you realize the story of Cain and Abel is actually the first murder in the Bible? It's the first time in history that one person chose to end the life of another person. And it all started with the seemingly simple sin of envy. Perhaps it's time to put down our envy and pick up our relationship with God. Envy distorts, but God is ready to bring clarity into our lives.

ALTERED

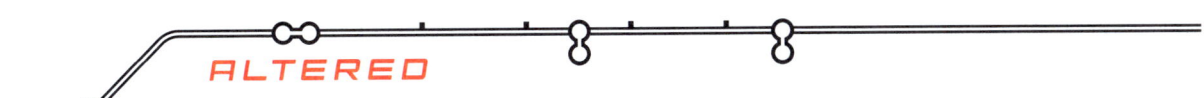

What's needed: *Music playing quietly* and *a few "confessional booths"* (see below) set up in corners of your meeting room

All that's needed to set up your "confessional booths" ahead of time are two chairs and some kind of curtain or divider to section off the area. Tell your students there will be one very important difference between these confessionals and the others your students have seen or heard about: these will be set up for an audience of One. They won't have a minister or sponsor in them. In fact, no other earthly person will sit in the other chair.

All that's needed is for a student to sit in one chair and talk to God, who's listening in the other chair. This may be a time to confess, a time to ask for help, a time to cry out . . . or whatever else they need.

For the students who may express that this feels "stupid" or silly: A reality that Christians believe is that God is omnipresent and aware of our needs at all times. It makes little difference, in other words, if we talk in the direction of an empty chair or a tree outside or bow our heads when we talk to God: Jesus is there. "And surely I am with you always," Jesus told us (Matthew 28:20). Encourage your students not to feel self-conscious but simply to focus on being honest with God and to experience the relief that that decision brings.

Play music so that students talking to God aren't overheard by others. Ask the students who aren't in a confessional to pray or talk quietly so they don't disturb those who are.

After as many as wish to participate have done so, end the night by praying for the group.

HOW TO KEEP FROM GOUGING OUT YOUR EYES (OR, FIGHTING FOR PURITY IN A CULTURE OF LUST)

WHAT IT'S ALL ABOUT

There is perhaps no more applicable lesson for students than a study on purity. You could teach on it each week for a year and still not exhaust the topic. We live in a sensual world, and it's getting progressively worse all the time. Don't shy away from this one; your students need to hear it.

Note: This is one lesson you will want to adjust in age-appropriate and gender-appropriate ways. Use your female leaders with the girls and guys with the guys. Teach, encourage, help!

Get It Started

What's needed: *A table; nine to fifteen Twinkie cakes* (but be sure to buy a number of extras beyond that total); *paper plates, paper towels; a small amount of ketchup, barbecue sauce, mustard, mayo, and horseradish, all in squeeze bottles; a spoon* to scoop out some of the cream filling; and *a prize* for the winner (a box of Twinkies is a fun choice)

Before students arrive, take these steps: prepare plates with three Twinkies on each. If you choose to have three students participate, you'll need nine Twinkies; for five students, fifteen of the little sponge-filled cakes. Be sure to have five or so extra Twinkies before you get started because there will always be casualties as you doctor up these little cakes.

Choose *one* of the Twinkies on each plate and, as gently as possible, scoop out as much of the cream filling as you can. Then, even more gently, replace it with another substance from one of the squeeze bottles. You can choose to create an assortment of filled Twinkies; you don't need to put the same thing in each one. Don't over-fill the Twinkies or they will burst and reveal their contents. (Once you've filled them with their new contents, you might even put some of the cream filling back on the bottom, just for sneaky fun.)

After one Twinkie on each plate has been filled with something gross, put them back and cover each plate with a paper towel so your students don't know what's coming.

Word to the wise: keep a large trash can near the table in case students end up quickly spitting out their lovely mustard-, ketchup-, or mayo-filled treat.

The activity: ask for three to five volunteers (depending on the number of plates you set up) for a Twinkie-eating content. (If your students have already been through the gluttony lesson, you may have to assure them that you have not done any research on government standards for insect filth in Twinkies!)

Tell them the game is simple: eat your three Twinkies first, swallow them completely, and get a prize. Then watch in enjoyment as students chow quickly on their Twinkies . . . until they find the one that you have doctored. Even when their faces start to twist with disgust, encourage them to keep going; there's still a prize to be won.

Once you've crowned a victor, use a segue like:

"Now, for those of you who ate the Twinkies, you may feel just a little cheated. There were extra things in there that you hadn't planned on, that I didn't tell you about. But keep this in mind . . . *nothing* I added to those Twinkies made them any less healthy. In fact, arguably, they were *more* healthy because I took out some of the cream filling and added other things!

"We fill our bodies, our hearts, and our minds with impurities far too often. Purity doesn't happen by accident. The only way we'll overcome lust and grow closer to God in the process is by being intentional about guarding what goes *in* to our minds and hearts."

Where It's Found in the Bible

Proverbs 4:23-27
Above all else, guard your heart,
for it is the wellspring of life.

Put away perversity from your mouth;
keep corrupt talk far from your lips.

Let your eyes look straight ahead,
fix your gaze directly before you.

Make level paths for your feet
and take only ways that are firm.

Do not swerve to the right or the left;
keep your foot from evil.

Matthew 5:27-30

"You have heard that it was said, 'Do not commit adultery.' But I tell you that anyone who looks at a woman lustfully has already committed adultery with her in his heart. If your right eye causes you to sin, gouge it out and throw it away. It is better for you to lose one part of your body than for your whole body to be thrown into hell. And if your right hand causes you to sin, cut it off and throw it away. It is better for you to lose one part of your body than for your whole body to go into hell."

YOUTH TALK OUTLINE

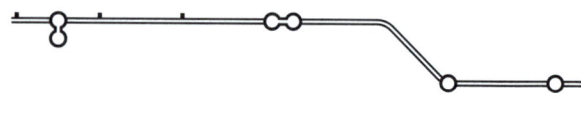

1. Know Your Limits

   a. The art of self-diagnosis

When you have a headache, what do you do? You go take some Tylenol, right? What do you do when your stomach hurts? You go take some Pepto, or something similar. It's actually easier than we think to diagnose problems in our lives. So why have so many Christians had patterns of letting their purity spiral out of control before recognizing there's a problem? Well, for starters, it's a difficult thing. Our sexual natures are comprised of God-given longings that were intended to bond us to our spouse.

Instead, we've settled for cheap substitutes.

BURST:

BRANDED:

Note: Again, it's best to have separate gender discussions for these parts of this lesson.

b. Guys

Guys, your struggle with lust is pretty obvious; it's all around us. Companies market to you like crazy. They blast you with sexual innuendos in commercials. They lure you with sensual images on billboards. And as though purity wasn't tough enough, now it seems like every movie hits DVD form with a No Rating label.

Let's call it like it is: people market to us like we're stupid. But we don't have to give in. And it all starts by recognizing the tricks Satan uses to weaken your defenses. Is the computer in a private place at home? Bad move. Work with your parents to move it to a place where you can't fall. It doesn't matter if other friends have computers in the room; are we listening to Jesus, our Lord, and taking his words seriously? Is your locker placed in just the right direction that you're seeing lots of girls? Start facing the other direction. Do your friends constantly make dirty jokes that you find yourself joining in on? What if you made Jesus the Lord of your life in this area as well and had three to four other topics you could change the subject to?

c. Girls

Girls are less visually oriented that guys, but girls, you are not immune to this temptation. Satan may not use the same tricks to lure you (and maybe he does for others), but he has plenty of tricks nonetheless. Are there posters in your room that should be taken down? Do you read romance novels that make you long for a guy that only exists in fairy tales? Are you texting guys about things that don't honor God in any way? You need to know your limits as well. Satan is on the prowl, looking for a way to get into your heart. Resist him at all costs.

Here's a great verse for both guys and girls:

Be self-controlled and alert. Your enemy the devil prowls around like a roaring lion looking for someone to devour. Resist him, standing firm in the faith, because you know that your brothers throughout the world are undergoing the same kind of sufferings [1 Peter 5:8, 9].

FOR DISCUSSION WITH YOUR GROUP:

Note: This is the only discussion set in this lesson, so spend some extra time here. Guys and girls need to talk about this topic freely—but they also need to hear and act on deep convictions.

- What are some of the tricks Satan uses to attack teenage guys and girls? (**Note:** Again, this can be an extremely helpful conversation for both genders to hear as long as you manage it, keep your genders separate—anything else is extremely awkward—and help keep the discussion appropriate.)
- How could we do a better job of encouraging each other to guard our hearts? Discuss dress, conversations, accountability, and more.

2. Avoid What You Cannot Handle

a. The Three Edwards

Lust comes in all kinds of forms.

Thomas B. Costain's history book, *The Three Edwards*, describes the life of Raynald, a fourteenth-century duke in what is now Belgium. Grossly overweight, Raynald was commonly called by his Latin nickname, Crassus, which means "fat."

After a violent quarrel, Raynald's younger brother Edward led a successful revolt against the duke. Edward captured Raynald but did not kill him. Instead, he built a room around Raynald in the Nieuwkerk castle and promised him he could regain his title and property as soon as he was able to leave the room.

This would not have been difficult for most people since the room had several windows and a door of near-normal size—and none was locked or barred. The problem was Raynald's size. To regain his freedom, he needed to lose weight. But Edward knew his older brother, and each day he sent a variety of delicious foods. Instead of dieting his way out of prison, Raynald grew even fatter.

When Duke Edward was accused of cruelty, he had a ready answer: "My brother is not a prisoner. He may leave when he so wills." Raynald stayed in that room for ten years and wasn't released until after Edward died in battle. By then his health was so ruined that he died within a year . . . a prisoner of his own appetite.[12]

If you hope to make some headway in your battle for lust, it begins with recognizing what makes you stumble. But you also must quickly move to avoid the things you know you cannot handle.

b. Girls

Ladies, it's important for you to learn this valuable life lesson today: In the world, girls give physical to get emotional; guys give emotional to get physical. And all too often what happens is that you get caught in dead-end relationships because you get so carried away with the idea of "being in love." Chick flicks, movies, and romance novels have sold you a lie. No guys will "complete you." There's only one relationship in this world that will meet all of your needs, and until you find him, every guy you date will fall short.

c. Guys

Men, this is an area where it's time for you to step up and lead. God has given you a role in relationships; it's time to own that role. The following words may be tough for you to hear, but you need to hear them anyway.

Pastors and spiritual leaders hear guys say things all the time like "But I just can't help it" or "This is how God created men" or "Why would I have these desires if I wasn't supposed to act on them?"

Men, it's time to answer a question: Are you a man or an animal? Do you have any self-control at all? If you're not still in diapers, then we refuse to believe that you have no control over your own body. Yes, God gave you sexual desire, and probably more than your female counterparts. You know why? He gave you those desires so that you would fall madly in love with your wife, spend your life with her, and keep the population going.

God doesn't ask you to protect your purity now because he wants to take your fun away. He asks you to prepare for marriage so that you can be the best husband in the world. Trust God: If you guard your heart now, you'll have better sex than you could imagine—and enjoy it for a lifetime.

BURST:

BRANDED:

3. Never Let Your Guard Down

a. From spring to waterfall

You've recognized your struggles. You're beginning to think through strategies to avoid what you cannot handle. Now it's time to live full steam ahead without letting your guard down along the way.

A great illustration of what lust and sexual impurity do in our lives can be found in rivers. Even the largest rivers in the world are fed by smaller tributaries. Somewhere in a remote place on the side of a mountain is a small spring which feeds into a creek, then into a river, and finally to a waterfall. Imagine your purity like this.

We start with something small like flirting. We like it, so we try more. One day we

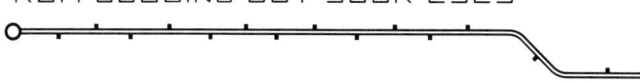

hold hands and get butterflies in our stomach. But sooner or later the law of diminishing returns kicks in and handholding doesn't do it anymore. We move on to a kiss, and so on. But with each step down the river, it gets harder to turn back. The current gets tougher and tougher to fight, and we find ourselves in some serious rapids. Eventually we come to a waterfall, and if we go over, we can never return again.

You have to make a choice to get out of the water at some point, or you will continue down that river until it's too late.

BURST:

BRANDED:

b. Girls

Accountability is key for both groups. Ladies, you need an accountability partner who will ask you good questions. You need to find someone you trust, can talk through each of your struggles with, and schedule weekly (or more often if needed) check-in times to see how you're each doing. You can pray for one another, encourage each other, and maybe say some tough things if it's needed.

c. Guys

Guys, desperate times call for desperate measures. You need accountability as well. Maybe meeting weekly with another guy will work for you, or maybe you need to take it to the next step and install some accountability software (X3 Watch is a current strong model) so that you have to answer regularly for how you're spending your time online. <u>Don't wait. Don't make the mistake of thinking you can win this battle on your own. That's one of Satan's oldest tricks.</u>

Wrap It Up

Go back to the words of Jesus. Is he Lord over your life or not?

Is guarding your purity easy? No. Will it require sacrifice? Yes. But think about it this way: how many of you have ever been on a sports team or in a play or production of some type? What does it take to be successful there? You have to give up things and make tough choices. You may not want to run, but it helps you condition. You may not want to spend time memorizing lines because you have other fun stuff to do, but that's the price you pay to get to perform.

What if we started looking at our future marriage that way? Preparing for it might require some sacrifices; it might mean that you give up some of the things your friends are involved in. But the payoff will be better than anything you could experience now.

ALTERED

What's needed: Nothing

Have your students close their eyes and process these final words.

"Ladies, listen to the following description of a woman of God in Proverbs 31 (verses 10-12, 15, 17, 20, 25-30). Are these the kinds of things you would like to have said about you?"

A wife of noble character who can find?
She is worth far more than rubies.

Her husband has full confidence in her
and lacks nothing of value.

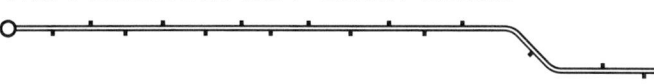

She brings him good, not harm,
all the days of her life.
She gets up while it is still dark;
she provides food for her family
and portions for her servant girls.

She sets about her work vigorously;
her arms are strong for her tasks.

She opens her arms to the poor
and extends her hands to the needy.

She is clothed with strength and dignity;
she can laugh at the days to come.

She speaks with wisdom,
and faithful instruction is on her tongue.

She watches over the affairs of her household
and does not eat the bread of idleness.

Her children arise and call her blessed;
her husband also, and he praises her:

"Many women do noble things,
but you surpass them all."

Charm is deceptive, and beauty is fleeting;
but a woman who fears the Lord is to be praised.

"Guys, some day you just might have a daughter. Think about the ways you look, dream, lust, touch, and fantasize. Someday, a world full of guys will want to do all of those things with your daughter. Spend a few minutes . . . thinking about that fact."

Allow these words to sink in for a few moments while students have their eyes closed.

End the night by praying for the group.

ANGER MANAGEMENT (CONTROLLING ANGER BEFORE IT CONTROLS YOU)

WHAT IT'S ALL ABOUT

Anger is all around us. Fights in schools, road rage, even oppression by one group over another. Rage seems to be all the rage. It appears as though we are becoming increasingly angry as a society, with no signs of it stopping. Why is that?

Perhaps the answer is . . . compromise. It's not that we're incapable of compromise; it's actually that we've compromised too much. When we compromise God's plan for our personal whims, when we compromise forgiveness for pride, when we compromise listening for lashing out . . . when we do all these things, we allow Satan to take over our thought processes. Rest assured, peacemaking is not something Satan is concerned with. We must sacrifice all of this anger for the sake of our relationships—both with God and each other.

Get It Started

What's needed: Have students *move their chairs to the side of your room*

Option: You may choose to put the questions and answers up on screen, but it's not necessary; you can simply read them aloud if you choose.

Begin with something like this: "Anger is an issue for all of us, isn't it? We're going to start today with a little anger management test. Be honest with your answers; there's no reward or punishment for finishing in the front or the back of the room.

"Start out standing as close to the center of the room as you can. I'm going to throw out some scenarios, and you need to take steps forward or backward according to your typical actions. Perhaps we'll find out who the peacemakers are among us—and who might benefit from a little class on anger management."

"I've been angry with at least one person this week."

One step forward if you have

One step back if you haven't

"I enjoyed the Adam Sandler movie *Anger Management.*"

Take one step forward if yes

Stay where you are for any other answer, including that you didn't see the flick!

Have you ever lost sleep because you were angry about something?

Yes—one step forward

No—two steps back

Someone cuts you off in traffic . . .

If you've ever followed someone in anger, two steps forward

If cussing or other gestures are involved in your response, one step forward

If you get annoyed but do nothing, stay where you are

If most of the time you keep total cool and even pray for the person, two steps back

You discover that someone at school is talking about you behind your back . . .

If you want to fight, two steps forward

If you go and talk about them behind their back, two steps forward

If you calmly confront this situation, one step back

Have you ever been in a fistfight?

Two steps forward if yes

One step back if no

(By this point, you may be wishing you had told the angry people to take steps backward if you're surrounded by anger management candidates!)

Have you ever stood up to boo a referee at a sporting event?

Yes—one step forward

No—two steps back

If your best friend had to choose one of two phrases to describe you . . .

Two steps forward if those words are *often angry*

Two steps back if *easygoing*

Have you ever been so angry you missed a meal?

Yes—one step forward

No—one step back

How long does it take to get over your anger?

A day or less: one step back

Two to three days: one step forward

If you often hold onto grudges for longer that that, three steps forward

Use a segue like (have a smile on your face and chuckle in your voice as you use these words): "Well . . . now we have a pretty good idea of the personality mixes of the people in this room! Those standing in the back are the ones you'd like to take with you if you're going on vacation. Those up in front are the ones you'd like to take with you if you're headed to a street fight in a dark alley!

"As funny as this activity was, the topic today is deadly serious. Anger is the cause of a lot of the problems and heartache we experience in our world today. People do and say hurtful things, relationships are damaged forever, and countries go to wars that could have been avoided . . . all because people refused to forgive and seek peace and, instead, allowed their anger to turn into rage.

"As you grab your chair and return back to the center of the room, let's see what Jesus, and the Bible, have to say about anger."

Where It's Found in the Bible

Ephesians 4:26, 27

"In your anger do not sin": Do not let the sun go down while you are still angry, and do not give the devil a foothold.

Matthew 5:23, 24

"Therefore, if you are offering your gift at the altar and there remember that your brother has something against you, leave your gift there in front of the altar. First go and be reconciled to your brother; then come and offer your gift."

James 1:19, 20

My dear brothers, take note of this: Everyone should be quick to listen, slow to speak and slow to become angry, for man's anger does not bring about the righteous life that God desires.

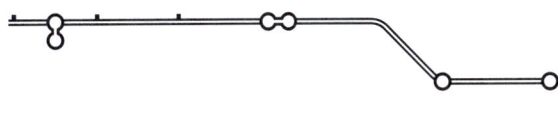

YOUTH TALK OUTLINE

1. In Your Anger, Don't Sin

a. The problem is sin, not anger

This may surprise you, but did you realize that anger itself is not a sin? Ephesians chapter 4 tells us not to sin when we're angry; it doesn't tell us to stop from ever being angry. Look at Jesus' example in John 2:13-16. He became so frustrated with the greed of the moneychangers in the temple that he went out, made a whip, and came back yelling and kicking them out. Do you honestly think Jesus wasn't angry while he did that? Of course he was angry. But there is more to the story . . .

Anger in and of itself is not a bad thing; what we do with that anger is. It's the same with lust. You can't help noticing attractive people as you walk along. What you can help is what you do with your thoughts after you notice. The next step is always the key. Anger helps us fight injustice, stand up for what's right, and stops us from settling for less. Road rage is a sin; being frustrated with reckless drivers who put others in harm's way is not.

FOR DISCUSSION WITH YOUR GROUP:

- What are some things that it might be OK to get angry about?
- What would be God-honoring ways to deal with anger in those situations?
- What are some areas of your life in which you struggle with unhealthy or sinful anger?

b. Don't let the sun go down

Paul teaches us a great lesson in Ephesians 4 when he tells us not to let the sun go down on our anger. Now, it's not always entirely possible to take this literally. After all, some married people might have to stay up for weeks at a time!

The principle is that we must deal with issues rather than allowing them to fester. No rational person likes confrontation. It's uncomfortable. It makes us turn colors. We have to be honest about feelings we'd rather bury. But it's necessary for us if we want healthy relationships and a mature faith. You have a biblical mandate to address issues, confront lovingly, and work toward restoration.

BURST:

BRANDED:

2. Anger Threatens Your Life

a. Anger threatens our relationships

During Jesus' many profound teachings in the Sermon on the Mount, he returns over and over again to the theme of love and forgiveness. There's a good reason for that. Have you ever noticed that when you're angry with someone, it affects everything else in your life? We get a crummy text message or e-mail and no matter how many other things go well throughout our day, all we can focus on is that one negative thing. Jesus tells us, in Matthew 5:23, 24, to stop pretending as if everything is just fine. If something's wrong, if you have a beef with a friend, go deal with it before you try to do anything else. That anger will affect every other relationship in your life, so it's critical that you address it now.

Are you holding any grudges? Are there people in this room you need to talk to? Are there people outside of this room who you need to seek out as soon as we're done today? Why wait? Why punish yourself and the other person? Life is too short to hold on to petty grudges.

BURST:

BRANDED:

b. Anger threatens our worship

As we've discussed in other lessons, you can't be consumed by two things. Our brains are powerful things, but they are not strong enough to allow love and hate to coexist. If you think you can worship God and hold a grudge, then you're fooling yourself. God is not honored by the lip service we pay him when we express love but live hate. The only way your vertical relationship can be all you want it to be is for your horizontal relationships to be all they're supposed to be.

FOR DISCUSSION:

- Which comes easier for you personally: grudges or forgiveness? Why?
- Have you ever held a grudge only to find out you were actually in the wrong about the issue?
- Why is it sometimes so hard for us to forgive?

3. Peacemaking as a Lifestyle

a. Two ears and one mouth

It's no mistake that God gave each person two ears for listening and one mouth for speaking. That's exactly what James is telling us in James chapter 1 when he says, "Everyone should be quick to listen, slow to speak, and slow to become angry." Making other people angry from time to time is inevitable. God made us all differently with unique gifts and skills and perspectives on the world. When two or more people share the same space, conflict is bound to arise. The question is: What will you do when it does arise? Are you going to go on the offensive, yelling and stating your case for the world to hear? Or are you going to choose peacemaking, the humble art of listening more than speaking? You don't get to choose how everyone else will react to you, but you *can* determine how you respond to them.

BURST:

BRANDED:

b. Righteousness

The rest of the verse we just discussed from James says: *"for man's anger does not bring about the righteous life that God desires."* Listen again, and allow those words to sink in: "for man's anger does not bring about the righteous life that God desires."

God has an amazing life planned for you—not necessarily easy, but amazing nonetheless! But it's possible for your anger to make you miss out on it. Webster's defines the word *righteous*, in part, as living "free from guilt or sin."[13] What if you could control your anger to the point that you never again had to experience guilt over poor decisions made while you were upset with something or at someone? <u>That's the kind of freedom God is offering if we'll just relinquish control and allow him to lead.</u>

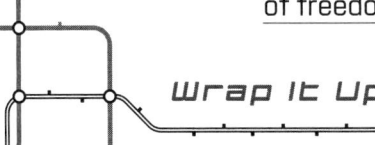

Wrap It Up

We can probably all agree that there is a lot of senseless violence going on in the world. But guess what? There is also a lot of needless strife occurring in your own life. Anger is addictive because it gives us a false sense of power, but that feeling is fleeting. When it's gone, it leaves a wave of broken and tattered relationships in its wake.

Don't allow anger to control you. Even if it feels like it helps in the short term, it will always make things worse over the long haul. God is offering you freedom if you'll just relinquish control and allow him to lead.

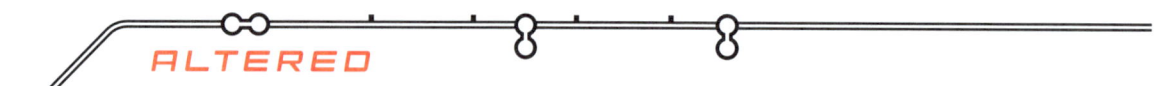

ALTERED

What's needed: *Construction paper and writing utensils* (pens, pencils, crayons, markers, etc.) for each person present; *envelopes* to seal letters in

Option: If you can have a small, safe fire pit or trash barrel fire outside, it will be even better and allow you to really cement this exercise.

Tell your students that letter writing is a timeless and proven technique for dealing with stress and releasing anger. Many times, if you're upset with one person in particular, the best thing you can do is to write a letter to that person and never send it. It allows you to get your feelings out and begin to move on without creating unnecessary confrontation and relational strife.

To close this meeting, your students are going to write a letter to God asking for his help. They may choose to begin the letter with something like "God, please help me to . . . " or anything else that seems comfortable to them. The point is to invite God to help them release their negative feelings, move past their anger, begin to forgive the other person, and seek forgiveness from God. And if the anger has been with God the whole time, this is a great opportunity to get that out on the table. Have them write the letter, fold it, and seal it in the envelope.

Note: Youth leader, you must decide *beforehand* what you want students to do with their letters once they seal them. Whatever you do, *do not* keep them to read later; that would be a significant breach of trust.

While allowing students to throw them into a fire is the most effective solution, if that's not an option, you can get a little creative. A paper shredder is probably the next best method, although the noise may be a little annoying. Or have them rip their letters up into little pieces and throw them out; discuss the freeing nature of this activity.

Fire pit option: If you do have a fire, wait until all the students have finished sealing their envelopes and then head out to the fire as a group. You may hold a brief, impromptu prayer service out there, praying for God to help everyone move past their anger and turn to him.

Then have your students throw their letters into the fire at one time.

Dismiss students after you've had one more short prayer and they've destroyed their letters.

GREED ROBS LIKE A THIEF (THE INTERSECTION OF FAITH + STUFF)

WHAT IT'S ALL ABOUT

This deadly sin is so much a part of our lives that we don't even notice it anymore. Credit cards, mortgages, student loans, car payments—none of it is bad in and of itself, but our addiction to stuff is taking us down. It's almost as though we're on the subway in some major city; our greed is robbing us just as a pick pocket would . . . and we're not even aware it's happening. We must draw a line in the sand and refuse to put material gain over spiritual gain in our lives.

Get It Started

What's needed: *a piece of paper and a pen or pencil for each person in attendance*

Option: If you have the tech setup (and the budget to buy songs), you may choose to create a playlist of money-related songs for this activity: "Can't Buy Me Love" by The Beatles; "Money for Nothing" by Dire Straits; and plenty more!

"How much do I spend on me?" That's the question your students are going to answer as you begin this session. Have them get into groups of two to three to help them think, although each person will be completing the activity for himself.

Tell your students:

"You have three questions to answer on your paper. And you're in groups so that you can each ask good questions and help one another think to reach good answers. The questions are:

1. How much money do I make in a month?

Now, we know what some of you are thinking: *But I don't have a job!* That doesn't mean you don't make money. Do you: mow yards, babysit, sell video games to friends, get an allowance, receive twenty dollars each month from your great aunt, etc.? We all make money in some way. On average, how much do you make in a month?

2. How much money do you spend on *you*?

iTunes, DVDs, dates, fast food, clothes, gadgets, the part of your cell phone plan that you pay, trips to the vending machine, coffees—whatever else gets spent on you.

3. What percentage of what you make do you spend on you?

(Even the non-math wizards should be able to do this one! Take the second figure and divide it by the first.)

In your groups, help each other think through every detail of income and expense. Accountability's always a good thing, right?"

When everyone finishes up, have a little fun by having your students share their percentages. You may ask everyone who's over 50 percent to stand, then remain standing if you're over 60 percent, and so on. (Avoid embarrassing any students, however.)

It might also be fun to find out who spends the *lowest* percentage on himself or herself. Again, just be sure not to poke fun at the students with the highest and lowest percentages; they are only being honest during this activity.

Where It's Found in the Bible

Matthew 19:16-26

Now a man came up to Jesus and asked, "Teacher, what good thing must I do to get eternal life?"

"Why do you ask me about what is good?" Jesus replied. "There is only One who is good. If you want to enter life, obey the commandments."

"Which ones?" the man inquired.

Jesus replied, "'Do not murder, do not commit adultery, do not steal, do not give false testimony, honor your father and mother,' and 'love your neighbor as yourself.'"

"All these I have kept," the young man said. "What do I still lack?"

Jesus answered, "If you want to be perfect, go, sell your possessions and give to the poor, and you will have treasure in heaven. Then come, follow me."

When the young man heard this, he went away sad, because he had great wealth.

Then Jesus said to his disciples, "I tell you the truth, it is hard for a rich man to enter the kingdom of heaven. Again I tell you, it is easier for a camel to go through the eye of a needle than for a rich man to enter the kingdom of God."

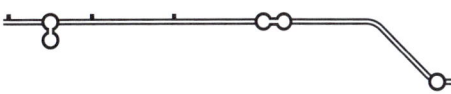

When the disciples heard this, they were greatly astonished and asked, "Who then can be saved?"

Jesus looked at them and said, "With man this is impossible, but with God all things are possible."

YOUTH TALK OUTLINE

1. Greed Robs Our Past

a. The Monopoly way

Did you ever play the game Monopoly as a kid? Many people did. In fact, many are still addicted to it! They're just too ruthless for anyone to actually want to play with them! Monopoly was a game that taught many people, from a young age, that the best way to get ahead is to climb on the backs of those around us. Who didn't like holding a five-hundred-dollar bill (back when that really meant something)? And landing on Free Parking, where you get the bonus cash (if that's one of the rules you played with).

While there's nothing wrong with the game, there is a problem when it becomes a way of life for us and we carry it into the real world. It's ironic that a game that arose as a reaction to the Great Depression of the 1930s actually taught many people the principle of greed and hoarding wealth.

FOR DISCUSSION WITH YOUR GROUP:

- Where do you see examples of greed in our world today?
- In what ways can teenagers be greedy?
- Where does greed enter your life the most?

b. Feeling like something's missing

There's an interesting attitude communicated by the questions the young man asked Jesus in this story. "What good thing must I do?" Or, specifically, "Which commandments do I need to obey?" Or, "If I've done everything right, what do I still lack?"

He's basically telling Jesus, "Yes, I've done all the right things my whole life, but it still feels like something's missing." It's easy for us to read the exchange and assume that either the man was arrogant or insane. How could he really have kept all those commandments? Well, for starters, the Jews in Jesus' day did a much better job of doing what God said than we do today; they were a very pious people. And when they did mess up, there was a whole system of atoning sacrifices to cover their sins. So this man wasn't arrogant or crazy; he was being truthful. He really had done most of the things in his life right. But he also knew something was missing from his life. That's what greed does. It robs our past by shortening our memory; we forget all that God has done because we can only focus on the things we want.

BURST:

BRANDED:

2. Greed Robs Our Present

a. The cost of ownership

Who owns whom? Do you own the stuff or does the stuff own you? That's the question we all must ask ourselves each day. In this story, the man's stuff clearly owns him. He asks for assurance of eternal life. He's asking Jesus what it would take for him to be able to sleep at night, to know that he's done all he can in his relationship with God. Surely, he's expecting to hear a dollar figure or some act of servitude that would set him apart—anything. His question is: "What good thing must I do to get eternal life?"

If you close your eyes, you could probably imagine the crowd watching and listening to all this take place. At the point that Jesus tells this man—who's obviously rich and well-educated by the way he dresses and speaks—that he must sell *everything* and give it to the poor if he wants to spend eternity in heaven, there must have been a gasp, a stunned silence, or both, that fell over the crowd. How could this be? In today's world, people would have looked at this man as a prime convert. *Get this guy as one of your disciples, and you can really leverage some serious resources!* But instead of staying on the surface, Jesus digs deeper . . . to the man's heart. It's a simple matter of ownership. Jesus knows that the stuff is weighing this man down, and his only hope of eternity rests in making God the number one priority in his life.

BURST:

BRANDED:

b. Giving is about trust

What would Jesus say to us if we were standing in the rich young man's sandals, asking the same questions? "So you're saying you can afford volleyball camp, but church camp is out of reach?" . . . "I've put it on your heart to support a child overseas, but you can't commit to the monthly donation. Wait, how much is your texting plan again?" . . . "You say you don't make enough to tithe. How is it you have enough to keep taking that girl out to movies then?"

Giving is about trust. If we're not giving generously, then it's because we don't trust God to take care of our needs like he said he would. We assume that we need to keep enough money around to be comfortable. What if God's not looking for you to be comfortable? What if God is tired of having a few comfortable countries and a globe full of hurting people? If you trust God with your money—which he gave you in the first place—then give more away and see what he does with it!

FOR DISCUSSION:

- Why is it a struggle for teenagers to give?
- How can you change that?
- Where are you doing well in terms of giving?
- Where could you be doing a better job of giving in your life?

3. Greed Robs Our Future

a. Camel / needle

There's a lot of debate about what Jesus meant when he said, "I tell you the truth, it is hard for a rich man to enter the kingdom of heaven. Again I tell you, it is easier for a camel to go through the eye of a needle than for a rich man to enter the kingdom of God." Some have even proposed that there may have been a "Camel's Gate" in Jerusalem in which camels had to drop to their knees in order to pass through. (The point is, according to this theory, that it took work, but the camels could do it.) Aside from there being no real evidence to support such a claim, there's a bigger issue—it totally misses the point. Jesus is painting a word picture. He used the largest animal of the day and suggested that it's easier for it to go through the smallest opening that people can think of than for a wealthy person to turn to God.

Notice that, Jesus doesn't say that you can't be rich and be a Christian at the same time. The Bible records plenty of godly people who were also blessed with significant amounts of money. The problem comes into play when someone who's tied to their money refuses to let go long enough to allow God's grace into their life. For the young man in our story, as rich as he was, the cost of following Jesus was simply too high.

BURST:

BRANDED:

b. What about me?

We ask the same questions as this young man all the time, don't we? We ask, "What do you want me to do?" Jesus answers, "You can never *do* enough." We ask, "How much do you want me to give?" Jesus answers, "No check will cover it." We ask, "Then what's it going to take?" Jesus answers, "I want *all* of you; nothing more, nothing less."

Jesus isn't looking for part-time followers; he's calling out for fully devoted disciples, for people who want to look and think and act like himself, the Teacher. He's asking you to cast away whatever hindrances might be keeping you from giving your all.

Wrap It Up

When money, when greed, takes hold, there are basically two camps in society. For some, it's not the stuff that's the problem. They give things away, and cheerfully. They'd give the shirt off their backs if someone needed it. They may even ask God to help them win the lottery so they can give *more* away. (As a side note, why would God help them win the lottery? He's seen what they've done with the smaller amounts he's given them; why would he trust them with more?) For those in this camp, the problem is actually the stuff they *don't* have. They need to hear 1 Timothy 6:10. Money is not the problem; it's their love for money that is.

The second camp may feel like they're trying to swim with a parachute on. The harder they try to free themselves, the more stuck they feel.

They're always worried people are going to take or break or misuse their stuff. They hold onto it, show it off, and always keep their stuff at the forefront of their minds. This group needs to hear Matthew 6:24—"No one can serve two masters." There will come a day when their stuff burns. They'd be better off to not be so closely tied to it.

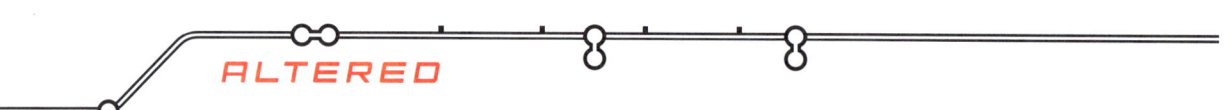

ALTERED

What's needed: *A one-dollar bill for each person in attendance*

Have students come to the altar, pick up their dollar, kneel to pray and ask for God's guidance, and then return to their seats. Explain to them that it's far too easy for us to allow greed to rob us of the good things God has done and is doing in our lives. But today, God's giving back. Each of them will leave with one dollar, and their task this week is to add more of their own and make a kingdom impact with their money. Ideas: maybe they will buy a few pops for a few friends, maybe they'll send the money away to an organization that will use it well, or maybe they'll come up with something else creative and effective to impact their community.

Close by telling your students: "Whatever the case, remember the story of Jesus and the rich young man. God's not nearly as interested in the gift as he is the heart of the giver."

End the night with prayer.

IT'S A BIG, BIG WORLD (WHATEVER IT TAKES TO DEFEAT SLOTH)

WHAT IT'S ALL ABOUT

When you boil it down, sloth is all about apathy. Sloth occurs when we don't care about the things God cares about—or maybe don't even care about anything at all. In either case, our own personal laziness prevents us from putting the things of God first in our lives. It's time to wake up a sleeping generation and inspire it to change the world in Jesus' name.

Get It Started

What's needed: *One dodgeball for each team* (put students in groups of eight to ten per team); and *you must have plenty of room to play this game, and dodgeball-proof the room—moving to a gym is best* if you can do it!

Today's opener is Dragon Head Dodgeball. Say what? Divide students into even teams of eight to ten. Send the teams to different corners of the room, and then have each team get in a single file line. Each person should put his or her hands on the shoulders of the person in front of him or her. Give a ball to the first person in line. They are now the "dragon head," the only person who is allowed to throw the ball. The person in the back of the line is the "tail," and they are the only one capable of being hit by a ball.

When another dragon head hits one team's tail with a ball, that tail person must move up to the front of the line and become the new dragon head. Once everyone on your team has been hit as the tail, your team must sit down where it's at and wait for the game to end. The last team standing is declared the winner.

You may want to remind the students—and it will probably need to be repeatedly—that they must stay connected to the person in front of them. If the team gets disconnected, they are not allowed to do anything else until they reconnect. If they hit another team's tail while disconnected, it doesn't count.

The point of the game is simple: the only way to win is to keep moving. You'll find that teams that get backed into a corner or take on a defensive strategy by curling around their tail will eventually lose. Do you run the risk of being hit if you're on the move? Yes. But you're an even easier target if you stand still.

Option: You can give these tips to the groups beforehand if you'd like.

One of the main points (along with, getting hit by a dodgeball can sting!): God didn't create us for laziness. God didn't create us to stay still. He created us to be active, on the move, and making a difference in our world.

Where It's Found in the Bible

Matthew 25:1-13

"At that time the kingdom of heaven will be like ten virgins who took their lamps and went out to meet the bridegroom. Five of them were foolish and five were wise. The foolish ones took their lamps but did not take any oil with them. The wise, however, took oil in jars along with their lamps. The bridegroom was a long time in coming, and they all became drowsy and fell asleep.

"At midnight the cry rang out: 'Here's the bridegroom! Come out to meet him!' Then all the virgins woke up and trimmed their lamps. The foolish ones said to the wise, 'Give us some of your oil; our lamps are going out.'

"'No,' they replied, 'there may not be enough for both us and you. Instead, go to those who sell oil and buy some for yourselves.'

"But while they were on their way to buy the oil, the bridegroom arrived. The virgins who were ready went in with him to the wedding banquet. And the door was shut.

"Later the others also came. 'Sir! Sir!' they said. 'Open the door for us!'

"But he replied, 'I tell you the truth, I don't know you.'

"Therefore keep watch, because you do not know the day or the hour."

YOUTH TALK OUTLINE

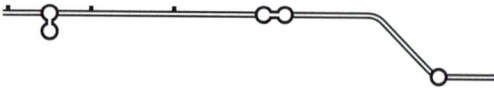

1. Are You Up and Moving?

   a. What were the other five thinking?

      Jesus' parable of the ten virgins most likely refers to ten bridesmaids who were waiting for the bride and groom to make their way to the banquet that followed their wedding. In a typical wedding of the day, after the ceremony at the bride's house, the bride and groom would head out on a parade through the streets to celebrate. The parade would lead to the groom's house for a banquet. It was the job of the bridesmaids to wait there for the bride and groom to arrive.[14] Five of these bridesmaids planned ahead and brought enough oil in case the processional lasted longer than they thought. The other five suffered from a lack of proper planning. We don't know if they were forgetful or just plain lazy. In either case, they weren't prepared when the groom was on his way.

b. Got Jesus?

It's important to remember that this story is told in a series of what have been called end times parables, meaning this is actually about Jesus' return, or second coming. The point is that we don't know the time or place of his return, so we need to live our lives in such a way that we're always ready. Sloth and laziness threaten readiness.

FOR DISCUSSION WITH YOUR GROUP:

- On a scale from 1 to 10 ("1" being completely lazy, "10" being constantly on the move), how would you rate yourself?
- When is it toughest for you to find motivation in life?
- When it is easiest to find motivation?
- What do you think is the real problem with laziness?

BURST:

BRANDED:

2. Multitasking Your Own Funeral

a. Trying to do everything accomplishes nothing

We live in a multitasking world, don't we? Any given evening you might be watching TV, listening to music through one ear bud, doing homework, surfing the Web, holding four different instant messaging conversations, texting a couple of your friends, and all the while pretending like you're actually listening to your mother when she's speaking to you!

But here's the problem. Our brains are not wired to handle the multitasking we put them through. Sure, we can all do more than one thing at a time, but that doesn't mean we're doing all of those things well. All too often, for all of our busyness and activity, we have very little to show for it. Sure you got your homework done, but did you really do it well? Sure you studied for that test, but did you actually learn anything? Sure you read your Bible, but did you actually get anything out of it? The more we do, the less we actually seem to accomplish.

Do we want to look back on our lives and see a bunch of sloppy tasks, finished halfheartedly, or do we want look back and see a list of accomplishments of which we're proud?

BURST:

BRANDED:

b. Wasting time

In our race toward inefficiency, coming in a close second to multitasking is our ability to waste time. Have you ever felt so stressed about all the things you needed to accomplish that you had a small meltdown and just zoned out watching TV or surfing the Web for an hour before getting to work? Our ability to waste time knows no bounds, doesn't it?

Now, we're not saying that hobbies are a bad thing. Neither are we saying that it's bad to take some time to relax or veg. Those things are actually helpful in living a well-balanced life. The issue is when we know we have important things to do, and we waste time instead. Or when we say we're too busy to read our Bible or pray, but we always find time to hang out on Facebook or text back to our friends.

Each of us must decide what our true priorities are in life and then ruthlessly go about working on those things until they're finished. Then we can enjoy much-needed and much-deserved breaks.

FOR DISCUSSION:

- Have you been guilty of multitasking to the point of getting little done well? What does that look like for you?
- What are the biggest time-wasting culprits in your life?
- What are a few things you could try this week to make yourself more productive and focused?

3. Refusing to Settle

a. This porridge is too hot, this porridge is too cold . . .

Jesus delivers a stinging reminder to us in Revelation 3:15, 16.

"I know your deeds, that you are neither cold nor hot. I wish you were either one or the other! So, because you are lukewarm—neither hot nor cold—I am about to spit you out of my mouth."

Halfhearted effort never pays off with God. He knows our hearts. It's time for us to commit, all or nothing, as followers of Christ. We simply cannot do this God-thing part-time. He doesn't need more slothful people; there are plenty all over this world. God needs more disciples who care about their families, neighborhoods, schools, communities, and world.

BURST:

BRANDED:

b. From apathy to accomplishment

People throughout the history of the world have made fun of every single generation of teenagers, calling them apathetic and lazy. But youth leaders today don't believe that about this generation. We know that you care about certain things. And we know that when you get on fire about something, nothing can stop you.

The hope and prayer for you is that you will never settle for less than your best. You're not sloths, moving in slow motion from branch to branch, never concerning yourself with what's going on in the world. You're on the ground, running a race, day in and day out. Let's pray together that God will awaken this generation and use it to change the world!

Wrap It Up

Go. Be God's hands and feet in this world. Be God's mouthpiece. Be a difference-maker. Sloth has no place in the kingdom of God because the news you have to share with the world is far too exciting and far too important. Sloth is about apathy. Instead, go and turn the world upside down!

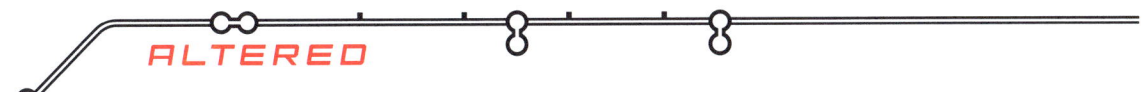

ALTERED

What's needed: Print off *one small picture of a sloth in a tree for each person in attendance*; *music playing quietly*

Give students time to reflect on this lesson. It's likely you've called them to a higher standard than they're already living. Give them some time to think, pray, and reflect.

When they're ready, invite them to come to the altar or front area and pick up a picture of a sloth. Ask them to tuck it away in a book that will be with them throughout the week; the picture should serve as a motivator. It will also act as a reminder that there's far too much to accomplish for God to allow laziness to keep us from living for him.

End the night with small group prayer.

[1] http://carriefisher.com/?p=30 (accessed June 4, 2009)

[2] Story used by permission of Emily Smedra to the authors and Standard Publishing, June 8, 2009.

[3] Bill Hybels, *Just Walk Across the Room: Simple Steps Pointing People to Faith* (Grand Rapids: Zondervan, 2006).

[4] Donald Kraybill, Steven Nolt, and David Weaver-Zercher, *Amish Grace: How Forgiveness Transcended Tragedy* (San Francisco: Jossey-Bass, 2007), p. 48.

[5] *Amish Grace*, p. 52.

[6] Mark E. Moore, *The Chronological Life of Christ, Volume 1: From Glory to Galilee* (Joplin, MO: College Press Publishing Company, 1996), p. 363.

[7] David Kinnaman and Gabe Lyons, *unChristian: What a New Generation Really Thinks About Christianity . . . and Why It Matters* (Grand Rapids: Baker Books, 2007), p. 28.

[8] Mark E. Moore, *The Chronological Life of Christ, Volume 2: From Galilee to Glory* (Joplin, MO: College Press Publishing Company, 1997), p. 207.

[9] Thomas Aquinas, edited by Anton C. Pegis, *Basic Writings of St. Thomas Aquinas: Man and the Conduct of Life, Volume Two* (Indianapolis: Hackett Publishing, 1997), p. 637.

[10] "Food Defect Action Levels," according to the U.S. Food and Drug Administration; http://vm.cfsan.fda.gov/~dms/dalbook.html (accessed June 11, 2009).

[11] "Fat Is the New Normal," *Science Daily*, August 7, 2007, www.sciencedaily.com/releases/2007/08/070806114259.htm (accessed June 11, 2009).

[12] Thomas B. Costain, *The Three Edwards: A History of the Plantagenets* (Popular Library/Warner Books, 1983).

[13] http://www.merriam-webster.com/dictionary/righteous (accessed June 12, 2009)

[14] Mark E. Moore, *The Chronological Life of Christ, Volume 2: From Galilee to Glory* (Joplin, MO: College Press Publishing Company, 1997), p. 203.